A Handbook On
HANGING

A Handbook On
HANGING

BEING A SHORT INTRODUCTION
TO THE FINE ART OF EXECUTION

CHARLES DUFF

The
History
Press

First published in 1928
This new edition published in 2011

The History Press
The Mill, Brimscombe Port
Stroud, Gloucestershire, GL5 2QG
www.thehistorypress.co.uk

British Library Cataloguing in Publication Data.
A catalogue record for this book is available from the British Library.

ISBN 978 0 7524 6068 0

Typesetting and origination by The History Press
Printed in the EU for The History Press.

Contents

Introduction to this Edition   11

Preface to the 1961 Edition   17

Fashions in Execution   21

English Neck-Breaking the Best   22

Praise for Hangmen   23

A Calm Consideration of Hanging   24

Hanging as a Fine Art   25

Hangman an Artist   26

Sheer Beauty of Hanging   26

British Hangmen Poor but Honest   28

Hangman a Man of Many Parts   30

Hangman a Brave Man   30

Hangmen Make Mistakes: John Lee   31

John Lee Saved by Rain!   32

To Err is Human ...   33

Open Competition and Examination for the Post   34

Charming Personality of Hangmen   36

A Uniform for Hangmen   37

Famous Libel Case Quoted   38

Conditioning for Hanging   40

No Ill-Will in Hanging   41

Bungled Hangings   42

Farcical Inquests and Official Secrets   44

Jurymen Must Demand Evidence   46

Fashions in Evidence   46

Is America More Civilized than England?   48

Broadcasting the Neck-Breaking   49

ANATOMY OF ENGLISH MURDERS   51

A GENERAL PICTURE AND THE DILEMMA   53

HOUSE OF LORDS A SURE PREVENTIVE OF ABOLITION   54

A HISTORY OF THE ANTI-HANGING CRUSADE   55

CAPITAL PUNISHMENT *ABOLISHED*!   56

ENGLISH HANGING "DONE ON THE SLY"   60

WHY NOT HANG IN PUBLIC?   60

MAKE HANGINGS MORE IMPRESSIVE   61

DECLINE IN HANGING   62

INCREASE IN LAW: DECREASE IN VIRTUE   63

VESTED INTERESTS IN HANGING   64

MERCY A DANGEROUS THING   65

CONSULT THE HANGMAN   66

DEAD MEN TELL NO TALES   67

CHANCE OF ERRORS REDUCED TO A *MINIMUM*   68

HANGING A "RITUAL SACRIFICE"   69

HANGING AND RITUALISM   70

EXTRAORDINARY CASE OF DEREK BENTLEY   71

THE WRITING ON THE WALL   73

PARTY POLITICS AND HANGING   73

MORE MISTAKES OF HANGMEN   74

FUN FOR THE HANGMAN   75

ALWAYS HANG WOMEN   76

ROMANCE IN A BUTCHER'S SHOP   77

A HYPOTHETICAL MURDER   78

THE END OF A DREAM   78

POPULARITY OF MURDER TRIALS   79

PLAN TO LOWER THE INCOME TAX   80

HANGED FOR SHEER STUPIDITY   82

A BOOK AGAINST HANGING!   83

DEPRESSING SIDE OF HANGING   84

A FAMOUS MODERN HANGMAN   84

THE GREAT HANGMAN INTERVIEWED   85

PRIDE IN PROFESSION   88

LOVE *VERSUS* CAREER   88

More Difficult to Hang one Woman
    than two Men!   89
A New Orientation in Capital Punishment   90
Executioners are Good Christians   91
Digression on the Nazis   92
Great Era of Execution   93
Royal Executioners and Aristocratic Hangmen   94
Executioners Risk their Lives   95
Drinking the Prisoner's Dope   97
Imported Hangmen   98
Sporting Instinct of the Greeks   98
Hangman who Hanged his Brother   100
On His Majesty's Service   101
The Press and Crime   101
Hints for Editors   103
Making Crime Pay   105
Memoirs of the Hanged   105
The "Hangman's Record" Quoted   106
Hangman's Magazine   107
The Pierrepoint Papers Quoted   109
The Condemned Man   111
Note on the Literature of Hanging   112
Hanging on Stage and Screen   113
Still More Mistakes of Hangmen   114
All Sorts Make Mistakes—Even Experts   116
Hangmen Not Concerned with Errors of Courts   117
Hanging in the U.S.A.   118
The Six who were Hanged   120
Death Never Instantaneous   123
Saving "L'Honneur de la Belle France"   125
Disgraceful Plagiarism Exposed   126
Electrocution is Torture   127
A Needle Through the Head   130
The Rosenbergs   131
U.S.A.: Abolition and Caryl Chessman   132

WIDER MORAL OF THE CHESSMAN CASE   134

THE DEATH OF CHESSMAN   135

UGLY STAIN ON CIVILIZATION   135

HONOURS FOR HANGMEN   136

WHO OUGHT TO BE HANGED?   137

GEORGE BERNARD SHAW QUOTED   137

PROFESSOR DR. JOAD, WIT AND PHILOSOPHER   139

THE GREAT NUREMBERG HANGINGS   140

DEFENCE OF A CHOICE HANGMAN   142

THE EXECUTIONER WHO WORKS FROM A DESK   145

ANTI-HANGING CAMPAIGNS   146

LORD TEMPLEWOOD ON HANGING   148

APRIL 1948: HOUSE OF COMMONS *AGAINST* HANGING!   149

HOUSE OF LORDS TO THE RESCUE   150

JUDICIAL PSYCHOLOGY   152

HANGING IN SUSPENSE   154

POST-WAR CRIMES—THE CAUSE   155

U.S.S.R—DEATH PENALTY ABOLISHED!   156

SOVIET DECREE OF MAY 1961   158

ROMAN CATHOLICS AND STATE KILLING   159

NOTE ON HANGING, DRAWING AND QUARTERING   161

HANGING, ETC., BULWARKS OF THE CONSTITUTION   164

ENGLAND'S OFFICIAL CHURCH FAVOURS HANGING   164

ENGLAND'S PUBLIC HANGINGS   165

THE BOLD FENIAN MEN OF OUL' IRELAND   166

ACCOUNT OF ENGLAND'S LAST PUBLIC HANGING   167

HANGMEN BORN, NOT MADE   169

HANGMAN'S VERSES FOR HIS CLIENT   171

THE *SCIENZA NUOVA*   172

A WICKED CALUMNY REFUTED   173

SPILSBURY ON THE DROP   175

HAND-IN-HAND WITH SCIENCE   176

HANGING, FLOGGING, WAR AND SADISM   177

THE LATE MR. BERRY ON HANGING   179

VITAL IMPORTANCE OF THE DROP   179

Mr. Marwood—Pioneer of the New Science   180
A Rough Working List of Drops   181
Doctor's Advice on Hanging   182
The Goodale Mess Explained   182
Doctor who Erred   183
A Hangman's Diploma   184
How Hanging Kills   185
Note on Pinioning   185
Note on Scaffolds   186
Hangman Describes Hanging   187
An "Order to Hang"   187
The Holy Procession   188
Last Scene of All   189
Those Last Fleeting Hours   190
Hangman Shakes Hands and Gets Busy   191
Fabulous Speed of English Hangings   191
Scaffold Unaffected by Progress, Revolutions,
     or Select Committees   192
Britain Stands by her Hangmen   193
The Last Certificate   194
The New Homicide Act of 1957   195
No Hangings: No Increase in Murders!   196
The New Sexual Offences Act   198
Campaign for More Hanging: 1960s   199
England's Defeat not Always a Victory   200
Homosexuality in England and France   201

Conclusion   203

Notes   205

Appendix: A Ready Reckoner for Hangmen   208

INTRODUCTION TO THIS EDITION

... [there is] no country on the face of the earth in which
there [have] been so many different offences according to
law to be punished with death as in England.

This was the opinion of Sir Samuel Romilly, in a speech on capital
punishment delivered in the House of Commons in 1810. His
statement is unsurprising considering the fact that in Britain at
that time there were no less than 222 crimes which were defined
as capital offences, including the impersonation of a Chelsea
pensioner and damaging Westminster Bridge. Moreover, the
law did not distinguish between adults and children, and 'strong
evidence of malice in a child of 7 to 14 years of age' was also a
hanging matter. For anyone found guilty of a capital crime, their
punishment was to be 'hanged by the neck until dead' and their
only hope of reprieve lay in the Royal Prerogative of Mercy.

As a form of capital punishment, hanging was introduced to
Britain by the Anglo-Saxons as early as the fifth century. William
the Conqueror subsequently decreed that it should by replaced
by castration and blinding for all but the crime of poaching royal
deer, but hanging was reintroduced by Henry I as the means of
execution for a large number of offences. Although other methods
of execution, such as boiling, burning and beheading were
frequently used in the mediæval period, by the eighteenth century
hanging had become the principal punishment for capital crimes.

The eighteenth century also saw the start of the movement
for the abolition of the death penalty. In 1770 William Meredith
suggested 'more proportionate punishments' for crimes. He was

followed in the early nineteenth century by Samuel Romilly and James Mackintosh, both of whom introduced bills into Parliament in an attempt to de-capitalise minor crimes. However, it was not until 1861 that the number of capital crimes was reduced to just four by the Criminal Law Consolidation Act, these being murder, arson in a royal dockyard, treason and piracy with violence. Further reform followed, and the last public hanging took place in 1868, after which all executions were carried out within prison walls.

Yet it was to be almost another hundred years before hanging was to disappear completely from the British justice system. On 9 November 1965 the Murder (Abolition of Death Penalty) Act suspended the death penalty for murder for five years in the United Kingdom and, on 16 December 1969, the House of Commons voted by a majority of 158 that capital punishment for murder should be abolished. Even after this the death penalty theoretically survived for treason, piracy with violence, arson in a royal dockyard and certain crimes under the jurisdiction of the armed forces, but with the ratification of the 6th protocol of the European Convention on Human Rights on 20 May 1999, all provisions for the death penalty were finally abolished in the United Kingdom.

Worldwide the death penalty is still retained in 77 countries as a way of dealing with a range of crimes. However, Charles Duff's satirical study of the 'humanity' of hanging and other forms of execution raises important questions as to the wisdom of a punishment which allows little room for error on the part of an eminently fallible justice system.

A Handbook on Hanging

Being a short Introduction to the fine Art of Execution, containing much useful Information on Neck-breaking, Throttling, Strangling, Asphyxiation, Decapitation, and Electrocution; Data and Wrinkles on Hangmanship; with the late Mr. Hangman Berry's Method and his pioneering List of Drops; to which is added an Account of the Great Nuremberg Hangings; a Ready Reckoner for Hangmen; and many other items of interest including the Anatomy of Murder by

CHARLES DUFF
of Gray's Inn, Barrister-at-Law

FINALLY DEFINITIVE EDITION DILIGENTLY COMPARED AND REVISED IN ACCORDANCE WITH THE MOST RECENT DEVELOPMENTS IN THE ART

All very Proper
to be read and kept
in every Family

"Executions are so much a part of British history that it is almost impossible for many excellent people to think of the future without them."

—VISCOUNT TEMPLEWOOD,
In the Shadow of the Gallows (1951)

"Dislocation of the Neck is the ideal to be aimed at."

"A hangman is an officer of the law charged with duties of the highest dignity and utmost gravity …"

—AMBROSE BIERCE

"By practice the art [hanging] is much improved and there is no part of the world where villains are hanged in so neat a manner …"

—*Gentleman's Magazine*

"The awesome shudder is man's finest attribute:
Even though by it the world makes consciousness cost more …"

—GOETHE, *Faust* II

PREFACE TO THE 1961 EDITION

It is pleasant for an author, however modest, to see a work of his appear, after over thirty years of marketing, in a new, greatly enlarged and enhanced edition such as this. It is now twice as large and, presumably, twice as good as it was on that September morning in 1928 when it was first given to the world. The reason for this lies in the perennial interest of the subject, as well as in the particular merits which the book is said to have.

The work of revision has been undertaken in no mawkish spirit, and it is hoped that a new generation of readers will find in these pages much that is educative (and perhaps even entertaining) regarding an English institution which retains much vigour after an existence which dates from long before 1066. Indeed it may be claimed without false modesty that here is the only book in the language which presents a comprehensive and well-focused account of hanging. Other books on the subject have their merits but, in my opinion, even when they are·better than this one, they do not treat either hanging or hangmen with the affection these both deserve. Furthermore, and this is a telling thought: hanging is likely to continue in England as long as there is a House of Lords. For the Lords Spiritual and Temporal still have the power to throw out, mutilate, or castrate any full-blooded measure which the House of Commons approves. This has happened; and, unless the House of Lords is reformed out of recognition, it must be expected to live up to its great traditions. The abolition of capital punishment is thus involved in constitutional change. And well it might be—in view of its long and usually steady history.

When the Germanic tribes of Angles, Saxons, and Jutes honoured Britain in A.D. 449 by invading it, they brought hanging with them, which upset the ideals of the Celtic Britons of those days. The gallows was an important element in Germanic culture. The worthy Hengist and Horsa and their colleagues used a very rough and out-of-hand method of hanging, one that resembled our clean and tidy modern method in only this respect: it worked quite well. In fact, it seems to have worked well enough for a millennium and a half: a remarkable testimony to its crude efficiency. In the nineteenth century the mechanics of hanging came under scientific scrutiny—it was a great age of science and progress—although there had been no public or private demand for it. Certain suggestions and improvements were adopted (you will read of them in their place) after which sweeping claims were made that the newly introduced trick for dislocating the neck was a vast improvement on the slower method of simple strangulation hitherto used. After the end of public hangings in 1868, the new science proved better for the greatly reduced company of those present at the ceremony: though not always better for the hanged person, even when it speeded the proceedings. There is a simple truth behind it all, and it is this: In spite of all the progress we have witnessed, even in our own time, it is not possible for the greatest physician, biologist, or any other scientist to define the exact moment when a hanged person, man, woman, or minor, ceases to feel pain. Nevertheless, the new method has many advantages over the old, one of them of political importance. Ever since its introduction those who commend hanging as a method of capital punishment have been able to put their hands on their hearts and make pro-hanging propaganda with a set of quite meaningless but very deceptive catch-phrases. One of these, for example, is that "*death by hanging is almost instantaneous.*" They make this claim in the sure knowledge that the unphilosophical man in the street will painlessly swallow the little word "almost" without ever realizing that, in relation to hanging, it can allow for a period of time which may not be more than two or three minutes, or it can be a quarter of an hour, or, as has happened, much longer. An intelligent law takes care of this in the sentence "to be hanged by the neck *until dead*." The operative words are "until dead."

In recent years a succession of disquieting instances of innocent men being hanged have come to light: Bentley, Rowland, and Evans are among them. These men were found guilty of murder, are now dead, and the attitude of The Establishment and of those who advocate hanging is that they must be considered guilty until they have been proved innocent. Although many extremely awkward facts have emerged in regard to these cases, final proof of innocence is hardly possible of achievement. Although these victims are out of sight, they cannot so easily be put out of mind.

So it is that, as these lines are written, campaigns for and against hanging continue. On this subject human nature is divided into two irreconcilable camps. It is unfortunately a political fact that hanging must depend on what political party is in power; apart from the obstinacy of the House of Lords—which can be final. Those who favour hanging claim that over 70 percent of the public is with them, and point to the results of polls. The subject arouses emotions one way or the other. And votes are important to the politically ambitious.

To my mind there is something much more important than votes: the difference between right and wrong. An important objection to capital punishment is that the logic of State killing of undesirables leads to Eichmann, the conveyor belts, and the genocidal gas-chambers. Killing is killing and constant familiarity with it breeds contempt or an immunity of feeling for killing. Capital punishment symbolizes an idea which on a parallel plane can logically end in press-button nuclear war: to obliterate the undesirable enemy. But, supposing that enemy can also engage in press-button war, what then? These things and their results cannot be separated from judicial hinging.

Meanwhile we go on; and hope for the best. Ours is a position of tragicomedy, the great tragicomedy of our time. As I so regard it, this final edition of *A Handbook on Hanging* has been expanded to include many items which I think of as relevant, because they are elements around the minor tragicomedy which is related to the major one.

I wish to thank my friend L.H. Hutchinson for his kindness in having read the proofs of this edition. And I must also record my gratitude to an anonymous American reviewer of an earlier edition who expressed his deep compassion for me in my own task of writing this Handbook.

C.D.

London, 1961

A Handbook on Hanging

Fashions in Execution

It has been, and still is, a matter of opinion whether, if you wish to kill your undesirable, it is better to let him die quietly in a concentration camp, flay him until he dies, hurl him over a precipice, burn, drown, or suffocate him; or entomb him alive and leave him to perish slowly in the silence of his grave; or asphyxiate him agonizingly in a lethal chamber, or press him to death or cut off his head; or produce a sort of coma by means of an electric current that grills him in parts and then, in the name of autopsy, permit the doctors to finish him off—as they do in certain of the United States of North America; or break his neck in strangulation by hanging as the English do. It is all a matter of taste, temperament, and fashion. But one fact emerges: man has not grown less cruel with the passage of that illusory thing called time; though in many parts of the world he has become a far greater hypocrite than he used to be. In the *Ts'in* Dynasty in China the heads of undesirables were expeditiously removed by a stroke of the official sword, whereas in the same country in our own century men and women had their ears and strips of flesh cut off, fried, and eaten before their eyes before execution; and children were ordered to behead their parents.[1] The methods of dispatch are without number and of infinite variety. The history of killing is the history of the world, and it is therefore hardly surprising to find that in nothing has man shown greater ingenuity than in inventing and perfecting methods and machines for killing his fellow man.

ENGLISH NECK-BREAKING THE BEST

The present work does not pretend to do more than touch the fringe of State killing, of which capital punishment is a less important aspect. Yet it must be accorded first place among State killings, because both gas-chamber genocide and the mass-obliteration of up-to-date warfare are the ultimates of its logic. We live in an awe-inspiring age, perhaps the "peak-point" of what is called Western Civilization: the age of atomic and greater bombs, of rockets, weapons worked by remote control, wonderful poison-gases and deadly bacteria which cost next to nothing to produce. What science is devoted to these arts of governmental homicide and genocide! How much of the most innocent and humane taxpayer's hard-earned (or even hard-fiddled) money is painfully extracted from him or her and, quite against his or her will, officially dedicated to research into the best forms of slaughter, carnage, poisoning (quick or slow, as may be required), asphyxiation, suffocation, paralyzation, atomization, and so forth in accordance with the imaginatively envisaged requirements of that great question-mark familiarly known as "The Next War." In certain circumstances an individual man or woman is ready to commit suicide: today we see what is euphuistically called our whole civilization deliberately preparing for suicide—all since the happy discovery by the great minds of science of atomic fission, and its reasoned utilization by the statesmen who have achieved power ostensibly because their peoples think that those statesmen are single-mindedly devoted to the public welfare. In A.D. 1960 the Americans claimed to have discovered a gas which with one whiff would paralyze the nervous system and kill *homo sapiens* in less than three minutes. This is an age in which the science of killing advances by great jumps. If those crude, rudimentary atomic bombs dropped on Hiroshima and Nagasaki taught a lesson to the multitude which they killed, mutilated, and sickened, what may we not hope for from the finer and more perfect weapons which men of science, subsidized and inspired by governments, are preparing? And preparing what for? Why, to make warfare more humane: by devastating whole areas, erasing most of their populations, and leaving only a select and favoured few samples of *homo sapiens* to survive and enjoy the problematical fruits which a wounded and man-poisoned earth may be able to produce. Pshaw! Here we can deal only with a midget portion of what is by comparison a trivial aspect of State killing: the elimination of the unwanted individual—a matter which tends to be overlooked in treatises of modern ecology and sociology. On this smaller aspect of the bigger subject I have collected what may prove to be useful information. For my own part, having carefully turned my thoughts upon the complex problem which it presents, and maturely weighed the several schemes of governments for the dispatch of criminals, I have reached the conclusion that no people can point to a method which is more beautiful and expeditious, or which is aesthetically superior to the time-honoured British practice of breaking their necks by hanging. It may be said that there is a fascination about hanging imparting an interest to details connected with it and its heroes which the best-disposed people in the community cannot wholly gainsay.

With the English the hangman is like the dog: the friend of man.

PRAISE FOR HANGMEN

Now this is an important fact which has not yet been impressed upon the world with sufficient cogency. I do, therefore, propose humbly to submit such relevant information as I have been able to collect in my leisure hours, and with it certain thoughts that have occurred to others as well as to myself: all of which, being calculated towards the general advancement of mankind, cannot be liable to the least objection. This short treatise is offered to a thoughtful public, in the hope that praise may thereby be won for the common hangman. Toleration he already has. After all, death is the least important event in the life of man, who is "immortal until his work is done," as everybody knows who reads about the casualties caused by motorists on the roads. There is an irony in life which becomes oppressive when we consider how some quite useless people live to be a hundred, while others are killed or mutilated in the prime of life by impact with vulgar automobiles. When the great chief priest of the people of the Congo fell ill and seemed likely to die, the man who was destined to be his successor entered the pontiff's house with a rope or a club and strangled or clubbed him to death:[2] which shows how philosophical a race of savages could be about death. An orange-peel carelessly thrown upon the pavement may take from us a great statesman, a great poet, a great painter; or a great public nuisance. An elephant may perish by a flea-bite in the ear. On the highroads, "*In the midst of life we are in death*," which truly is fortuitous in so many instances that it seems to be a matter of very small concern how or when it comes. The evidence shows that hanging is as effective as any other form, and certainly less messy and less painful and more reasonable than being turned into raspberry jam on the deadly highways of civilization.

A Calm Consideration of Hanging

Taking this as a basis it is possible to write calmly on the general subject of State execution, and especially in its most beatifying form. One may consider hanging from various points of view. One may, for example, treat it as the most interesting of the fine arts. One may weigh its aesthetics, or consider it as sublime; or ridiculous. One may even take hanging as the unit of morality, and delve into the history of hanging. Yet although it is an ancient practice, hallowed by its very antiquity, it is not my intention to write an erudite chronicle of suspension, but rather to deal with it as it is today and to offer suggestions for improving it generally, and thereby to increase its well-deserved popularity in this England which we love.

Where *all* authors have failed hitherto in their treatment of hanging is that they have never for a moment considered hangmanship as a fine art: as, for example, the Japanese have regarded the ceremonial swordmanship they employed when conferring a special honour on the person decapitated. Our writers have not considered all that goes towards making a good job of it. They have omitted to mention a thousand and one aspects of the subject which are of interest to the moral philosopher, and also of interest to all those who are in any way concerned with hanging, from the hemp-picker who collects the raw material for making the hangman's rope to the grave-digger, who prepares the secluded resting-place of the man, woman, or infant who is hanged. It is my intention to attempt to remedy these grave omissions, and indeed to offer a serious if brief contribution to contemporary thought on the whole subject.

HANGING AS A FINE ART

Let us begin then by considering hanging as a fine art.

We may almost assume that it is a fine art, and not a base mechanical trade. Is not a man an artist who can painlessly and without brutality dispatch another man? There is a certain delicacy about the operation which needs a ready eye, a swift-working brain, cool and calculating, and a clever touch which is only to be found in the realm of the great arts. The architect constructs a great building from a significant series of outlines; the musician constructs an entire symphony from a series of tones; but our hangman by one pull of the lever achieves more than either. A great American critic has stated that art of the highest or finest quality involves three things. First, a reproduction of natural phenomena; second, an expression of the thoughts and emotions of the artist; and, third, an embodiment of both these features in an external product, like a symphony, a poem, a painting, a building, or a statue. Or a hanging, I would add.

HANGMAN AN ARTIST

The hangman is also an internationalist, in the sense that he would just as soon hang a white man (or woman) as a black, a foreigner as an Englishman, a Nordic as a Jew. Furthermore, he is pantheistic: for he would as lief hang a member of the Church of England as a member of the Roman Church, a Four-Square Gospeller or any other true believer, pagan, agnostic; or even an atheist. One cogent reason for this detachment and impartiality is that he gets the same professional fee for breaking any sort of neck. He is, in fact, an honest working man, a proletarian elevated to be an official, in the fullest Marx-Engels Leninist-Stalinist sense. One must confess that it is a little puzzling to know whether it would be correct to classify him under the heading "proletarian," for at times he has decidedly *bourgeois* and even aristocratic taints. So we had better, once and for all time, simplify matters by putting him in the non-descript category of artist. Thus, we may avoid hair-splitting political arguments and, at the same time, render *some* justice to a great Servant of the State without giving the least offence to anybody.

SHEER BEAUTY OF HANGING

It is, of course, true that hanging is, like script-writing for the films or television, an art in a class by itself. But it is one without the discords of other arts. Large numbers of people are by nature excluded from the sphere of action of the artist, and so it is impossible for them to appreciate the aesthetic paradise in which the hangman lives. I confess I find some difficulty in conveying an impression of this, just as I should find difficulty, though in a lesser degree, in conveying an impression of certain of William Blake's poems. The critic or commentator is always at a disadvantage in a description in mere words of an art in another medium. The beauty of hanging is recognized by its effects on the mind, just as the beauty of a Velazquez painting is recognized in the same way; and we must be content to leave it at that. Benedetto Croce calls art *intuition*. Who amongst us cannot immediately recognize *by intuition* that hanging is an art, and the executioner an artist? Hanging has all the characteristics of art: conservatism, the elaboration of an instinctive mode of expression, balance, harmony in effects, rhythm, tone; and effect. Nor is it over grown by modernist fads, fancies and "cranky" ideas—no need to introduce into it surrealist influences, Dadaism, Existentialism or what not. It works admirably without them. There is no need to labour this point unduly; though I may have to refer to it later. But here I should state that the *beaux arts* never reveal their full possibilities in a country which is not wealthy, and in which men may not devote their time in a leisurely manner to the pursuit of the beautiful. (I think Plato or Wells—or both—made this clear.) One of the chief reasons why England is supreme in hanging is because in this cultured land hanging has always been regarded rather as a spare-time employment of a cultural nature than as utilitarian means of livelihood. Many hangmen were barbers—that is, since barber-surgeons were separated into two distinct callings. Our quite recent Hangman-in-Chief Mr. Albert Pierrepoint (a descendant of the Huguenots?) keeps a public house; and a very pleasant host he is by all accounts. His favourite assistant at hangings, Mr. Harry Allenby, is also a publican. As might be expected, both have not only a sense of humour but of the fitness of things, for the name of Mr. Pierrepoint's merrie hostelry was "Help the Poor Struggler,"[3] while that of Mr. Allenby is pleasantly named "The Rope and Anchor"— the word "Anchor" being used in the symbolist sense. In the 1950s some of the more enlightened members of the American Army of Occupation in Britain made their pilgrimages to these outstanding and friendly hostelries, where libations could be offered to the good-hearted hosts and their hangmanship. There is one thing which, I frankly confess, still greatly puzzles me and has so far defeated *all* my researches. I cannot explain why it is that so many of the hangmen of England have been and are of the Unitarian persuasion, though I have noted that most of these Unitarians show their common humanity towards the about-to-be-hanged by a last-minute assurance that "It won't hurt," sometimes varied thus:

"It won't hurt a bit." Could anything be more Christian or, for that matter, more humane? The scaffold *does* unite lost souls.

BRITISH HANGMEN POOR BUT HONEST

The office of hangman has never yet received its due either in praise or in rewards from the public. Until 1952 our English hangmen were paid fifteen guineas (*guineas*, not pounds, proving recognition of their professional status) for each person killed; and the perquisites are now negligible. In 1952 their remuneration was increased by an amount not yet disclosed, though we all hope that it is more than the increase in pensions then awarded to disabled ex-servicemen, for it could hardly be less. Hence, the hangman's post in Britain is not like the post of Public Executioner in the United States of America, where a Mr. Elliot went out "to make his million." In the United Kingdom there is an average of about 150 cases of murder known to the police every year. Of these only 90-100 are proceeded against, and in only about twenty-five are there actual convictions for murder. Why, not a baker's dozen of human beings is executed every year! It will be seen from this that, unless the emoluments of the English hangman were very high, or at all events brought with them substantial perquisites, the public executioner could never hope merely by virtue of his office to become a rich man. Although this may be in the best tradition of the Government Service, you must agree that it is deplorable. Even if pay and conditions for hangmen have improved in recent years, it is appalling to think how bad they once were. I see in The Times of 30/1/1794 this shocking statement:

> A petition from Wm. Brunskill (commonly called Jack Ketch) was presented to the Court of Aldermen stating that he was the public executioner and, on that account *could not get any other employment* (my italics); that he was obliged to keep an assistant, though his allowance

was small, and *his income so trifling* (again my italics),
as to be insufficient to maintain himself and family; and
praying relief.

Very terrible, and not like now when hangmen are so loved
that they can keep a pub. Our contemporary neckbreakers' and
stranglers' honoraria are based on the usual Treasury niggardliness,
which is deplorable always—except for special (and usually
political) appointees, when it can be really generous—but
particularly deplorable in the payment of hangmanship. It is all
the more deplorable when we compare the delicate art of the
hangman with that of the "electrocutioner" or the guillotiner, or
the garotter of other countries less civilized than Britain. What
skill is required to operate a switch? What skill is required to twist
a garotte? What skill is required to decapitate with the aid of an
elaborate engine? I do not include in the same category as these
three the German method of beheading with axe or sword. Thank
Heaven there is still some art—or rather science—remaining on
the continent of Europe. The Germans used to go even further
than we do in recognition of their science, for their executioner
performed his ceremony in evening dress, like a violinist playing
a symphony to an enraptured audience at the Wigmore Hall, or
any other *virtuoso* appearing at a public function. The English
hangman performs in a lounge suit; or, for all I know, in plus-
fours. He certainly does not function either in evening dress or
even a smoking-jacket, though in Scotland he has before now
worked in kilts, and I hear that some of the moderns have taken
to wearing a black coat and waistcoat and striped trousers just like
many diplomats, higher Civil Servants, lawyers, and the smarter
undertakers. But mostly public executioners wear a bowler hat and
a dark suit—like collectors of outstanding accounts, writservers,
bailiffs (or bums as they are frequently called), and other modest
personalities of our times and culture. In private life he looks just
like an average man—which, of course, he is *not*. This shows how
casually the English treat the business.

Hangman a Man of Many Parts

To return to the vexed question of art.

Before a man is hanged, the hangman has to assume the parts of a mathematician, a scientist, an engineer, and an expert in dynamics. Combined with these he must have the mind of a philosopher and the soul of one who practices art for art's sake. This must be so, because he is so inadequately paid that nothing but the subconscious drive which impels great artists towards their major achievements could otherwise account for his choice of this greatly underestimated and deplorably unrespected profession. Here I would dwell for a moment upon this most delicate aspect of the hangman's calling. I mean his pay and social status.

Hangman a Brave Man

Owing to the increased cost of living he has not received from the public which he serves one-hundredth of the consideration of which he is worthy. Art is all very well; but the artist must live. Apart altogether from the artistic side of the question, a man must be a brave man to be a hangman. I do not mean physical bravery, but moral. And I do not mean moral bravery in the sense that he need have any qualms or pangs of conscience in regard to hanging anybody; but that a great deal of moral courage is required to face the loathing, disrespect, and even hatred of an ignorant and inconsiderate public. Not that there are not some people who regard him as what he truly is: a hero and an artist. Fortunately, we are not all depraved, and one was glad to note a recent move to treat the hangman as the image of Sublimity, with reference to the Absolute; though this is probably exaggeration.

But I must not wander away from the main thread of the subject. Having measured the man to be hanged, taken his weight, examined the contours of his neck (and felt its muscles), the hangman who has a job of work on hand must next see that his apparatus is in good working order. This may appear a simple matter, but it is not really, as you will learn later. If he omits to see to the oiling of his lever and bolts and also the hinges of the trap-door upon which his subject is to stand, he may easily bungle the whole thing. And this has happened. There was one man, a certain John Lee, whom they could not hang; a sort of sport in the game who refused to succumb either to art or mechanics; either to argument, persuasion or virtuosity.

Hangmen Make Mistakes: John Lee

John Lee is a great figure in the annals of hanging—so important that his life, like that of the King of Kings, Nero, Joan of Arc, etc., proved interesting enough to be filmed. Alas, the film was a bad one, and omitted the most entertaining aspects of the hero's adventures (I fancy the censor may have cut them).

He possessed the secret, if not of eternal life, then of prolonged life. He refused to die, and it is necessary to say on behalf of the late Mr. Berry, who officiated at the long drawn-out hanging process, that he was in every way qualified to perform the task. To judge from a perusal of his highly instructive book of titillating reminiscences, Mr. Berry appeared to possess something like an ideal mental equipment for the line of work he entered upon. He had a keen eye for tone and a just appreciation of the bearing of his art upon human conduct. He had graduated in the university of wide practical experience and had all the tricks of the art at his finger-tips. But the cruel fact remains. Three times he tried to hang John Lee; and three times he failed. Unhappily, no record was kept of what Mr. Hangman Berry said or thought when he found that John Lee had bested him. It was a humiliating position for any English executioner and one can well imagine him saying the words used in Matthew xxvii, 46. Let us hope that the hangman was adequately paid for his extra work and the frustration in this case, for there are few sadder pages in the history of the art than this tragic failure. Neither the spirit nor the flesh of the hangman was weak; though it is clear that both spirit and flesh of John Lee were strong. I take this opportunity of vindicating the honour of the great State Strangler whose services were retained for the dispatch of John Lee. Any man who imputes weakness either to the executioner or to the governor of the jail or to the warders, or to the priest of God who was paid by a considerate Government to minister to the last spiritual needs of the man to be hanged, will certainly have to answer to me. There was an exaggeration of terseness in Mr. Berry's style which was often a great excellence. No flaw or hitch could be discovered in the whole business. John Lee simply won the game, feet down. It has been suggested to me that the failure to deal adequately with John Lee is a proof provided by Providence of his innocence. Maybe. I incline rather to attribute it to immunity from hanging developed by heredity in accordance with Mendel's theory; and I would also submit it as a fact tending to prove the correctness or otherwise of the Darwinian theory of evolution.

In the U.S.A. great powers of endurance and survival were shown by a Mr. Purvis whose survival of a hanging enabled his friends and lawyers to produce evidence of his innocence. This was a terrible thing for the State to face. Good Will Purvis survived the jurors who found him guilty. The State, of course, cannot lose face in such cases, for the simple reason that the State is faceless: a wonderful convenience for what is now called The Establishment. Then again there was an interesting Mexican case: Wenceslao Moguel was not only shot thoroughly by a firing-squad but was given the usual *coup de grâce*. He lived to exhibit himself at the "Odditorium" Fun-Fair on Broadway for $75 a week. His public had good value: his benign countenance was scarred and bullet-ridden. But this is considered to have proved nothing, for many men have survived a firing-squad in modern totalitarian conditions.

John Lee Saved by Rain

The failure to hang John Lee was officially explained as due to rain which had caused the planks of the trap to swell. That might well have been the case: but, if so, it indicates grave negligence on the part of the responsible authorities in not having chosen either well-seasoned wood or at least a good timber which would not easily absorb water, as this did. They are more careful today. But there are still three or four schools of thought among experts as to which wood is best for gallows, the better thinkers being in favour of teak. It is a small problem, and unimportant, especially as we may soon have a streamlined gallows made of plastic. Collectors, antiquarians, and curators of museums may be interested to know that the actual rope used in the classic failure to hang John Lee, together with holograph letters written by Mr. Hangman Berry, were in 1948 exhibited for sale in a Nottingham junk-shop. Whether or not they have been snapped up by a shrewd investor, I do not know. Incidentally, John Lee lived to a ripe and contented old age.

To Err is Human ...

Now the chief object of this illustration is to show that hanging is an art, and not a mechanical affair. In a mechanical business such as guillotining or garotting, or even electrocution, there could be no such failure, though it must be admitted that the history of electrocution is not also without its black pages. It is recognized that an art may fail by its own inherent weakness, and this is not a bad example. It is not the only case on record in which the art of hanging failed. One can still pick up in the second-hand bookshops old prints which show that, on occasion, the hangman had to climb upon the gallows and finish off his victim by jumping on his shoulders. And I have heard of cases in recent years in which the hangman had to descend into the gallows-pit, seize his victim by the feet, and, with a sharp and expert tug, break his neck. It is only fair to the art of hanging to mention these bunglings and miscalculations, though they must not for one moment be considered as any indication of failure of the art as a whole. And they must not be advanced as arguments against it. I have no doubt whatever in my own mind that John Lee could have been brought to a satisfactory end had the authorities permitted the hangman a few further attempts. I should put the limit at thirteen. After all, however artistic a hangman may be, he is human and bound to fail sometimes:

To err is human, to forgive divine

—a sentiment which, if rather old-fashioned, is not too platitudinous to be cited here. I have another authentic case of a failed hanging: that of Ronald Seth, whom the Germans tried to hang as a spy in German-occupied Talinn in Estonia during the Second World War. Mr. Seth survived to report:

> The trap on which I was standing suddenly gave beneath
> my feet, fell a few inches, and then stuck. I heard shouts,
> and saw blurred figures running hither and thither. Then
> I fell forward. The rope tightened behind my ears, and
> my eyes were filled with bright lights and then darkness.
> It was early afternoon when I came to and found myself
> back in Cell 13.[4]

The failure was this time due to vodka, of which the guards drank more than was necessary to warm them in that cold climate. Some anti-Germans took advantage of the alcoholized state of the guards to "fix" the gallows and, when it came to the ceremony, the trap stuck, the crowd jeered at the officer in charge, and, fearing a rescue, he himself rescued Ronald Seth before he died. It was a near thing. However, this case can be dismissed as one far out of the ordinary, and unlikely to happen in Britain, where our alcoholic drinks are more modulated in manufacture.

OPEN COMPETITION AND EXAMINATION FOR THE POST

This brings me to the qualifications of a good hangman.

The case of John Lee happened within living memory and is in the nature of proof that not nearly enough care is taken in the selection of our hangmen. At present they are appointed by the old and discredited system of patronage, and it seems to be a specially "reserved" occupation and no "direction of labour" applies to it. In the ordinary British Civil Service patronage was abolished very many years ago. A competitive examination or choice selection now decides who shall be important Civil Servants, and I would suggest that the competitive method be applied to the office of hangman.

That the competition would be keen I think there is no doubt.

I submit that if a small advertisement were inserted under "Public Appointments" in any of the great newspapers or periodicals the Civil Service Commissioners would be overwhelmed with applications. In his own time the late Mr. Berry was one of 1,400 applicants when a vacancy occurred. Research indicates that States can find executioners even in circumstances when one might think it impossible. The authorities in the French penal settlement in the Iles de Salut (Salvation Isles in English) found a convict who, in return for modest privileges, would execute his fellows in tribulation, although he thereby became the most loathed man in the settlement. *Pecunia non olet*. Imagine the thrill in Kensington and Hampstead and Mayfair on reading these words:

> A competitive examination will be held between the 1st and 14th of August next for the post of Public Hangman in England. The successful candidate will be expected to undergo two years' probation before definite appointment. Commencing salary will be at the rate of £900 10s. 10d. per annum, plus Civil Service bonus at the current rate.[5] Canvassing of Cabinet Ministers or Members of Parliament will disqualify. Forms of application with Birth Certificate to be sent in before the 31st May. The standard of education will be that of Pass B.A., Durham University; but a knowledge of arithmetic will be expected. The successful candidate must have a high moral character. Women may compete in this examination. Only natural-born British subjects need apply.

If there was a rush of applicants for the post, the governing motive would not necessarily be a pathological desire for notoriety, though it might be—we have seen many examples of such a desire. But I have such faith in the patriotism of the average Englishman that I am certain there would be a shoal of applications. It would, indeed, be necessary to damp the ardour of many pathological enthusiasts, and no better way could be found than to make the examination as difficult as possible. A high standard would have to be attained in mathematics and science, as well as a keen appreciation of art and the humanities. Subtle problems could be set on the arithmetic of drops. Here is an example of the type of question I have in mind:

> You have to hang Mr. A. He is 5 ft. 10½ in. in height and weighs 12 st. 2 lb. 6 oz. 1 dwt. His neck from the Sternocleidomastoid to the Sternohyoid measures 6¾ in. The neck is strong and 17 in. in diameter. Calculate to three places of decimals the drop necessary to hang this man thoroughly, without risk of giving pain to onlookers. Also give the diameter and quality of the rope you would employ, in terms of pounds avoirdupois of strain.

Charming Personality of Hangmen

It is essential that a hangman should be a person of wide culture and sympathies. He ought to be able to take his place in any grade of society, and above all things he should not be too class-conscious. During the Second World War, and after, he had to travel as a Very Important Person mixing freely with other V.I.P.s. He ought to be capable of being the philosopher and friend of whomsoever he must hang for us. He ought to have "personality" in the stage sense of the word; be able to "put it across." It is difficult to say what a hangman ought not to be, except callous. That would be unpardonable and intolerable from the point of view of the British public, the Queen's Government, the Christian religion, and our daily and sabbath Press. He ought also to have a good working knowledge of anatomy and a little psychology would do no harm. There is no reason why one human neck should not be as regular as another, but experience has shown that no two are the same; and hence the hangman must move cautiously. Mostly he is a person of great discretion and charm whose art produces a unique and delightful personality. He ought to have a good practical knowledge of railway travelling so that he could, without loss of time, keep his appointments in different parts of the Kingdom. At a pinch the public hangman ought to be able to drive a motorcar or fly an aeroplane, ride a horse or bicycle, and be a good after-dinner speaker. All these things would add to the dignity of his office and overcome the ostracism to which it has so unworthily been subjected in the past. Is not the executioner a conceptualist? The government department concerned ought to, and does, I think, provide him with a fully printed List of Instructions for the performance of his difficult task; and there should always be at least two understudies, fully qualified, and not less than six probationers (*Henkersknechte*), to assist him.

A Uniform for Hangmen

Another idea which occurred to me was that a uniform should be devised for the public hangman in England, as for certain other branches of the State services: the Army, Navy, and Air Force, for example, which are employed for the killing or maiming of foreign enemies in time of war. In time the public would grow to love and respect the uniform of the hangman, just as they now love and respect the uniform of other persons in Her Majesty's employment. Are not the London police regarded as marvellous and is not their uniform highly esteemed? Who does not adore the bright trappings of the Guards Regiments or indeed of the gentlemen who stand outside picture palaces or great hotels? Women would soon learn to "fall for" the public executioner, who would become as much sought after as a crooner or film star. It has indeed been a very complete mystery to me and to my friends why no uniform has been given to so exalted a personage as the hangman—especially when one considers all that is meant by the word "uniform."

FAMOUS LIBEL CASE QUOTED

This brings me to a matter which may as well be dealt with, before proceeding further. I have often thought that it is a disgrace to our whole system of justice that the judgment in a case of slander (quoted by the *Law Journal* of 28th August, 1926) has not been reversed. The facts of the case were somewhat as follows: On the night before an execution at Norwich, a respectable citizen got out at a hotel. So ultra-respectable was this gentleman in appearance that the bystanders took him for His Majesty's hangman. An onlooker cried aloud in joy, "You are ——" and mentioned the hangman's name.

"Not I," replied the respectable citizen.

"Yes, you are," persisted the ordinary citizen, and with that the mob, either incensed by the respectable citizen's cheeky attitude or feeling in a mood for a lark, threw the respectable citizen into a duck-pond. The victim of this outrage decided in his own mind that the man who first took him for the public hangman was responsible. He consulted a lawyer and sued the originator of the assault for damages for slander. There was no doubt of the special damage; but the defence pleaded by way of demurrer that the allegation could not possibly be defamatory.

> "The executioner," said the defence, "is a public official necessary to the security of the State, and it is no more a libel to describe a man as an executioner than to say that he is a judge."

Now this case, like all cases, was tried by a judge, and a judge like every other human being upon this earth has his own private virtues, failings, prejudices, animosities, likes and dislikes, loves, hates, complexes, neuroses, emotions, and so forth, as listed by the trusted psychoanalyst. Few indeed are the judges who can, at a moment's notice, suppress their entire personality and become a sort of abstract automaton capable of pouring out judgments that are entirely without bias and devoid of prejudice. For some reason (which I fail to explain) the judge in this particular case rejected the contention of the defence and held that the charge of being a hangman was calculated to bring its victim into hatred, ridicule, and contempt, and therefore—if not in fact justified as true—was undoubtedly actionable as defamation.

Thus, it is an extraordinary truth that a Court of Law in Great Britain has badly "let down" one of its most important and praiseworthy auxiliaries. What was really wrong about this case was the entire *mentality* of the Court. I live in hopes that this Handbook will go a long way towards a clarification, a purification, and a general rectification of such mental *malaise*. The defence might have been, on the other hand, a little more subtle. They could have said, for instance, that instead of it being a slander to call a respectable citizen the public hangman, it was rather a slander upon the hangman to confuse his appearance with that of a respectable citizen. The epithet "respectable citizen" is not nearly good enough for so important a personage. It is as though one had called the great Lord Curzon a "respectable citizen" when the world acknowledges that he was much more. This erroneous judgment must be reversed, though our present hangmen are so modest and retiring by nature that the occurrence of an occasion to justify bringing a case into Court is remote. Incidentally, there is no friendly society or protective association for executioners nor even a trade union, for this would be *infra dig*. At the same time, it must be admitted, there remains the feeling that every error has its element of truth; and in this case the Court of Law may have been right.

Let us now consider for a moment the ceremony of hanging, and if possible put forward suggestions for the improvements that could easily be made in it. Never has fortune favoured me to witness a well-ordered hanging; though the late Mr. Hangman

Ellis performed it delicately in a play at Gravesend and in a private booth on the sands of Yarmouth, where, for the modest expenditure of sixpence, one could see how well he worked. Incidentally, he was a great admirer of this modest treatise on his art—he once signed a copy for me, and sent several copies to friends as Christmas and birthday presents—though there are parts of it which did not meet with his whole-hearted approval. But that is by the way.

CONDITIONING FOR HANGING

A prisoner who is condemned to death is "received" by the governor of the jail in which the hanging ceremony is to be performed. Warders have instructions to give the convicted man special attention, special nutriment, his preferred tit-bits, favourite cuts from the joint, some extra tobacco; and what not. For his amusement dominoes are provided; and no other game, not even tiddlywinks. As for reading matter, there is the prison library with its selection of good books including The Bible and Shakespeare. What more could a man want? Every effort is made by the chief warder and his associates to make the unfortunate man happy. Sometimes they succeed; mostly they do not. However, I am not greatly concerned with the condemned man, but rather with the system, for it is the system that can be improved. The death of an individual is a trifle when we think of war and the general slaughter and butchery that is synonymous. To repeat what was said earlier, when we think of the atomic, bacterial, etc., war that may come, what is the death of even the most important individual? And cannot death itself, even death by execution, be made, and frequently is made, into an admirable thing? I need say no more on this aspect of the subject but to remark (with many eminent living theologians and divines) that Christianity itself might not have taken its great hold upon the imagination of the world if Christ had not been executed. Out of evil good can come; and the end justifies the means. Now let us return to the prison and the condemned man. A hangman is commissioned. One day he arrives, bag in hand, with the tools and equipment of his great art. He visits the prisoner, passes the time of day, looks him over with a skilled all-seeing eye, measures him, weighs him, examines his neck and makes a mental note of its strength, presumably looks at the prisoner's tongue, and having asked him to say "ninety- nine," enters it all in a notebook specially kept for the purpose. Bidding the prisoner *au revoir*, he sometimes (as the late Mr. Berry used to do) handed him a religious tract, or a few lines of verse specially composed by himself to meet the circumstances of the case. This is no longer permissible. Who knows what the nation loses by the unjust suppression of the poetic impulse in our hangmen? Just think of the modern verse we are losing! I intend some day to take up this question with the Poet Laureate. And it has been called "atrocity"! Having studied his notes (and worked out the correct drop) he is ready to hang the prisoner as soon as they wish. No trouble about that. The *St. James's Gazette* provides a simple description of what happened on the morning of an execution, as recounted by an eye-witness:

No Ill-Will in Hanging

"Calcraft was the executioner. He was a bearded veteran who had been educated in the fine old school of hangmanship. As usual, he took the business businesslike, and pinioned his man in his cell (with a terror-stricken half-dozen looking on) as calmly to all appearances as if he had been a tailor fitting on a coat. The chaplain read the Burial Service, or such portions of it as are reserved for these occasions, in a thick and indistinct voice." (He may have taken something to sustain his courage during the proceedings.) "The doomed man gabbled a prayer under his breath at galloping speed, the words tumbling over one another, 'Lord Jesus, have mercy on me, and receive my spirit.' The hapless chaplain read the service. Calcraft bustled ahead. The bell boomed. Hughes (i.e., the prisoner) came to the foot of the gallows, and I counted mechanically nineteen black steps, fresh tarred and sticky. A genial warder clapped him on the shoulder, for all the world as if there had been no mischief in the business. Judging by look and accent, the one man might have invited the other to mount the stairs of a restaurant. 'You'll get up all right,' said the warder.

"He got up and they hanged him.

"So that's that, was the attitude of all."

This is a plain account, unvarnished and without the ornamentation which a sentimental writer like myself might be tempted to add. It was a straightforward job, artistically and competently carried out to the satisfaction of Her Majesty the Queen and all members of the Royal Family. To the entire satisfaction of the members of both Houses of Parliament; of the Archbishop of Canterbury, chief representative of the official religion; and last but not least, it was carried out to the satisfaction of the whole British public, excepting a few cranks and faddists who, almost from time immemorial, have uttered querulous protests against this extremely important aspect of public policy.

BUNGLED HANGINGS

Mr. Hangman Berry—his name is already familiar to the reader—like most men prominent in public life, amused his old age by writing a most delightful book called *My Experiences as an Executioner*. It is a great classic, and I shall have to refer to it again and again—perhaps one day I shall bring it out in a new edition with variorum notes. I mention it here because he tells of one case of his, the hanging of a man called Goodale, at which the prisoner's head was jerked right off the body. Hangmen and other government officials concerned with executions in Britain still speak of this with awe as the "Goodale Mess," and one of their terrors is that, because of some slight oversight, it can easily be repeated. To avoid anything so unseemly a man named William John Gray, sentenced to death for the murder of his wife, was reprieved quite recently—in April 1948, to be exact.

After shooting his wife, Gray shot himself, fracturing his jaw. Medical examination showed that the injuries caused were of such a character "as make it impracticable to carry out the execution." The prison authorities were convinced, the Press was told (*News of the World*, 4/4/1948), that Gray could not be hanged "without extreme physical agony." This could mean one of two things: that he might die from strangulation because of a failure of the brass eyelet to cause dislocation; or that, to cause dislocation, he would have to be given a drop so long that his head might be pulled off. Hence, in the interests of both humanity and hanging, it was *much safer* to grant him a reprieve. An interesting case. But to return to the "Goodale Mess." There was something wrong somewhere, and of a hangman so great as Mr. Berry[6] I should not have believed this story had he not very honestly related it in cold print. Possibly he did not observe the unities; even Shakespeare neglected them at times. You will remember that it was Mr. Berry who tried three times to hang John Lee. One hour and eleven minutes were taken to hang Antonio Sprecage in Canada, 1919. These are very sad incidents in the history of the art, but they will never recur if my recommendations are accepted by the Government. In 1927 the British Medical Journal published another account by an ex-colonial surgeon of a botched hanging. He stated that he had to witness the execution of four coloured men (natives, no doubt). The executioner was in a hurry that day to keep another appointment, and decided to hang these four men in pairs. It must be admitted that in the case I will now cite there was a certain lack of balance on the part of the hangman. The highest beauty results from harmony in effects; and one cannot say that in this case the combination of thoughts and feelings was harmonious. I shall give the good surgeon's own words:

> When the first pair were hanged it was my duty to determine the fact of death. As a general rule, on auscultation the heart may be heard beating for about ten minutes after the drop, and on this occasion, when the sounds had ceased, there was *nothing to suggest a*

vital spark. The bodies were cut down after fifteen minutes and placed in an ante-chamber, when I was horrified to hear one of the supposed corpses give a gasp and find him making spasmodic respiratory efforts, evidently a prelude to revival. The two bodies were quickly suspended again for a quarter of an hour longer. The executioner, who was thoroughly experienced, had done his part without a hitch, and the drop given was the regulation one according to individual physique. Dislocation of the neck is the ideal aimed at, but, *out of all my post-mortem findings, that has proved rather an exception, while in the majority of instances the cause of death was strangulation and asphyxia.*

Note the words emphasized.

Farcical Inquests and Official Secrets

Now it will be acknowledged that this sort of muddle and bungling, for it was nothing else, plays havoc with the aesthetics of hanging; and puts it on a level with crude execution in the cannibal islands. In saying this I may be libelling the cannibalistic executioner, who is often a priest of religion, and no doubt a most conscientious man on such occasions. I can in my imagination hear many readers say: "Ah, that was a long time ago. Hangmen do not make such a mess of things in our enlightened age." So-hoh! Do they not? I have before me a clipping from a Canadian publication called the Hush Free Press dated 16th February, 1946. I quote from it:

Private Bruce Potter, aged 47, a one-time American soldier, murdered Mrs. Edna Ina Rogers at Dawson Creek, Peace River, Canada, last summer. He was apprehended, tried, found guilty, and ordered to be hanged by the neck until he was dead, and may God have mercy on his soul.

On January 10, 1946, that sentence was carried out by an official hangman in the presence of official observers at Oakalla Prison, Vancouver; the prisoner mounted a gallows, had a rope fastened around his neck, and was dropped through a trap, in the usual way. But apparently the hand that tied the rope was somewhat lacking in science and skill. Apparently the victim was decapitated by his fall; some people who saw the body afterwards declared that the head was torn from the trunk. Now defence counsel has stated his intention to bring an action of some kind against the hangman.

How shocking this mess must have been for the official observers and the unfortunate hangman! And in civilized Canada! Something must have gone wrong somewhere. I should like to make it clear on behalf of the sheriffs of England, of prison governors and, above all, of our present generation of hangmen, that there is no *great* likelihood of *their* making such a mess of things. I say no great likelihood, though it must not be ruled out as an utter impossibility: I have already drawn attention to the haphazard system now in force of appointing hangmen, and there is no guarantee whatever (as there might be after appointment by open competition and examination in the manner I have already suggested) that the hangmen are *in every way* qualified for their task. It should be noted that, in accordance with instructions issued by the Home Office to prison governors in regard to what they may say at inquests on men that are hanged, the rule is that death is always *almost instantaneous*. Caution demands the word "almost." Mark you, a governor is forbidden to time an execution. He must not have a stop-watch in his hand while it happens. Should an *inquisitive* coroner or coroner's juryman press for details of how the hangman has done his work, *the governor must hedge*. In accordance with the explicit instructions he must say, "a very short interval elapsed," or some general expression of opinion to the same effect![7] There is no logical reason to quibble about this because the judicial sentence is: "To be hanged by the neck *until dead*"—and therefore an hour or so one way or the other does not really matter, so far as the law of the land is concerned. After the drop, the body is left hanging quietly for at least half an hour, which nearly always suffices to complete the killing.

JURYMEN MUST DEMAND EVIDENCE

In the interests, not of Justice, but of that equally important thing the hangman's art, it is difficult for any of us who have this at heart to sympathize with official suppression of useful information. In the United States of America the whole business would be made clear in a closely reasoned report, with interesting tables of comparative statistics as an appendix. We must all do our utmost to erase, from the otherwise clean record of capital punishment in England, such regulations as this, for they tend to keep from the columns of the daily Press, and therefore from public discussion or even scientific inquiry, vital information regarding the act of hanging. Social progress is hindered, the paths of science and art are obstructed; and prison governors are placed in a false and, some would say, utterly dishonest position. A verdict is recorded; an apathetic public looks on, and the world jogs along somehow. That great institution the Coroner's Court is placed under an official anaesthetic, and the inquest is an insult to the dead body, to the jury, and to the solid common sense of the English. When shall we have a jury that will stand upon its undoubted rights and *demand evidence* from governors and witnesses? Otherwise let us completely abolish inquests on executed felons, and thus clear our minds of cant.

FASHIONS IN EVIDENCE

Evidence in trials of persons who may suffer the penalty of death if found guilty is, like capital punishment itself, largely a matter of fashion depending upon time and place. What is and what is not evidence finally depends upon the Court; and judges pay great attention to precedents. The American writer Ambrose Bierce (whose works are greatly neglected) has this to say: "As records of courts of justice are admissible, it can easily be proved that powerful and malevolent magicians once existed and were a scourge to mankind. The evidence (including confession) upon which certain women were convicted of witchcraft and executed was without a flaw; it is still absolutely unimpeachable. The judges' decisions on it were sound in logic and in law. Nothing in any existing court was ever more thoroughly proved than charges of witchcraft and sorcery for which so many suffered death. If there are no witches, human testimony and human reason are alike destitute of value." Bierce had a fine sense of things, as his definition of the gallows indicates: "A stage for the performance of miracle plays, in which the leading actor is translated to heaven. In this country (U.S.A.) the gallows is chiefly remarkable for the number of persons who escape it." As regards the last comment, I think he is rather hard on his fellow-countrymen, who have no monopoly of this form of good fortune. Bierce is aware of the fact, for he quotes with approval a notable epigram of the learned and ingenious Dr. Jamrach Holobom:

> In each human heart are a tiger, a pig, an ass, and a nightingale. Diversity of character is due to their unequal activity.

Capital punishment Bierce regards as "a penalty regarding the justice and expediency of which many worthy persons—including all the assassins—entertain grave misgivings." It would be deplorable if, in these pages, the fact were omitted that Ambrose Bierce wrote a not irrelevant or irreverent masterpiece with the title *The Monk and the Hangman's Daughter*, an elevating story of spiritual values not always conflicting. Apropos, there was a long period of the God-fearing days of the Middle Ages during which animals were publicly tried and, if found guilty of the heinous charges in their indictments, duly executed—by hanging among the variety of ways recorded. A classic was written on the subject. But as, in spite of anything that can be said to the contrary, in this book we are dealing with human beings, we cannot spare space for the poor animals. The story of *their* sufferings could hardly be borne by an animal-loving people such as the English. One must apologize for the omission.

IS AMERICA MORE CIVILIZED THAN ENGLAND?

In the good old days of public execution—in the heyday of hangmen—the public was able to judge for itself. The deliberate official suppression of details is wrong from another point of view. In the first instance, if execution is intended to frighten potential criminals into virtue—and that is its avowed object—why is it not done publicly as in France? Secondly, why, if it must be done behind closed doors, is there not at least a properly equipped Press gallery, with desks, telephonic facilities and so forth at the disposal of newspaper reporters? Again we must look to the excellent example of the United States. At the execution of a Mr. Grey and a lady known to posterity as the "Iron Widow," there was not sufficient accommodation in the death-house for the gentlemen of the Press. The authorities did the only thing that was fair in the circumstances—they admitted the Press in relays. One enterprising journalist even took a snapshot of the lady in her deaththroes as she sat in the "chair." Knowing how interested the American public is in such matters, the editor of the New York *Daily News* gave it full-page reproduction. What a scoop this was! Copies of the newspaper were, as might be expected, greedily snapped up. Very soon the whole edition was sold out and the news boys were clamouring for additional copies. The sales made a record. The picture was eagerly sought by connoisseurs; it was even catalogued under *Facetiae* in the list of second-hand booksellers.[8] There is something touching about all this which makes one feel how much we are losing in Britain, not to mention the purely financial losses to those distinguished peers of this realm and others in the newspaper business who are ever willing to provide us with the kind of news we like best. It is a public scandal. I may add, by the way, that after this execution, Mr. Robert Elliot, the "electrocutioner," had to take to his bed. It is not quite certain whether his indisposition was caused by killing overwork or by nervous exhaustion as a result of being over-interviewed by enthusiastic and sympathetic admirers, like royalty after a day's handshaking. This is a thing the English must guard their hangmen against. Nobody fully realizes how exhausting interviewing can be to the one who is interviewed. We should therefore see that our hangmen are provided with a welltrained Public Relations Officer, who would not only relieve them of much tedium, but would see that the right sort of material, whether "human interest," anecdotal, informative or straight propaganda, was issued to the Press. Have the patient British not a right to demand proper hand-outs on hangings? These are generously distributed on almost every other subject under the sun and fill the waste-paper baskets in Fleet Street. They do things better in those efficient United States. Take, for example, the efficiency of the publicity given to the electrocution of Mrs. Creighton, romantically called "New York's Borgia Killer," in July 1936. Cables were hot conveying to the four points of the compass the news that, for three days before her execution in Sing Sing, she had been so paralyzed with fear that she was "unable even to feel needles thrust into her body and was unconscious when lifted from a bath-chair into the electric chair." Sing Sing certainly must have an excellent publicity service—not much happens in it that Americans cannot read in their fine morning papers. Do not think for a moment that this pamphlet is a subtle piece of American or other propaganda; or an attempt to advocate American methods. But let honour be given where it is due, and let us also frankly recognize that we are not respected for our hole-and-corner hangings.

BROADCASTING THE NECK-BREAKING

In spite of the obstacles placed in their way by a grand motherly Home Office, it must be admitted that English newspapers are not entirely bereft of the spirit of enterprise. Did space but permit I could quote many *excellent* morsels of news published in recent years. This is all to the good of hanging, but it must be confessed that with a proper provision of Press facilities there is no reason why the great art should not be relieved of the gloom of darkness which now surrounds it; and in the course of time even become a deterrent to murder. Personally, I see no reason why the more important hangings should not be broadcast by wireless, just as a great fight is broadcast; or any other exciting event. The crack like a muffled shot of a small pistol which indicates the official breaking of the criminal's neck ought to be broadcast; when the neck is not broken, listeners would hear the "squelch"[9] of strangulation—which would give equal satisfaction to many and tell its own story. Ex-hangmen could be employed by the British Broadcasting Corporation to provide colour and background to the details and noises transmitted through the ether. They might even be commissioned to give us an occasional twenty minutes' Talk in an egg-head programme on so intensely interesting a subject. In Britain it would have to be a straight Talk, but in the United States it could in some places (where hanging holds the field against electrocution) be a sponsored programme, and possibly interspersed with advertising for rope, dope, and other consumer goods such as we see on television. This would be a remunerative sideline which, added to fleeting appearances on the legitimate stage, to interviews on occasions when somebody is about to be or has been hanged, to the writing of Memoirs for the more religiously minded of our Sunday newspapers, and to the reviewing of books such as this, would fully occupy the retirement of public executioners, and give them that meed of life in their old age which their gallant self-sacrifice rules out while they are holding office. As one who has the interests of hanging greatly at heart, I devoutly pray that the day is not far distant when the cinematograph, television, the three-dimensional phono film, the wide screen, glorious colour photography, and other ingenious inventions of this enlightened age, will be pressed into the service of the public to bring home to Mr. Everyman a just appreciation of the nobility of the hangman's art. How instructive it would be to see a good British hanging film inspired by J. Arthur Rank, produced by some clever genius like the late Sir Alexander Korda, and, best for this purpose, directed by an artist like my friend Fritz Lang, with scenario by a Winston Churchill, script by a good team, additional dialogue by T.S. Eliot, O.M., further additional dialogue by Mr. J.B. Priestley, still further supplementary additional dialogue by anybody who happens to be on the film company's pay-roll and doing nothing, with hanging details by a Pierrepoint, and if possible supervised by a Home Office official who knows all the secrets and, God help him, could perhaps keep the film people within the bounds of common sense. We deserve a soulful and imaginatively spectacular film of an English hanging in this Year of Our Lord. By sending out to the world a work of epic grandeur dealing with capital punishment as it is ordered and inflicted, Old England could show those backward countries where it has been abolished how truly backward they are. A great missionary work could thus be achieved, and we should gain for an uneasy Exchequer a vast quantity of dollars. I trust that some enlightened and influential person will put this idea to those who frame the National Budget. As the subject illustrates an English way of death, it is for the British Council to include it in the British way of life which the Council explains and propagates from Tierra del Fuego to Timbuktoo, in the *salons* of the *élite*, and among top people and even among those who hardly matter in the select places of the earth. In 1949 the British produced a most amusing film about a hangman, *Kind Hearts and Coronets*. It was a little on the frivolous side, yet it showed the screen possibilities in this truly wonderful subject. Why is it so neglected?

ANATOMY OF ENGLISH MURDERS

No people are more consistent in the quantity and quality of their murders than the English, a fact which must be noted and always borne in mind while thinking of hanging. Statistics prove this consistency to the hilt.[10] For example, the annual rate for the first half of the twentieth century was 3.89 murders per million of the population. And now

MURDERS KNOWN TO THE POLICE: STATISTICS

	1930–39	1940–49	1950–54	1955–56	1957	1958	1959
Number.	131	167	141	148	166	137	149
Per million of the population	3.6	4.4	3.7	3.7	4.2	3.4	3.7

Could statistics be more eloquent? These official figures dispose out of hand of the hysterical claims constantly made by that mentally floating part of the population which can decide the result of a general election. In emotional moments, following some particularly brutal murder, shrieks go up for a return to the good old days of more hangings such as we had before the introduction of the Homicide Act of March 1957 (for which see page 239 later). These well-meaning but often silly or ignorant people maintain in fact if not in actual words that the English people are becoming more murderous than they were in the past, and even assert that with fewer hangings we must have more murders! This simply is not so, as any hangman worth his salt will tell you. There has been very little change in the English, a naturally conservative people, in this and other fundamental respects. Our human nature maintains the even tenor of its way, whatever the hysterics may wish to claim. And their claims about murders and the effect of hangings are not only based on false premises. They are unworthy of a great people who are both keystone and cornerstone of modern western culture and civilization, such as these are. Campaigns for and against hanging, since this book was first published, have become important elements in the warp and woof of social life in this England. The unsatisfactory compromise known as the new Homicide Act (1957) was both the end of one pair of such campaigns and the beginning of another. As these lines are written (Spring 1961) one more pair of campaigns is with us, which inspired *The Observer*[11] to publish a valuable "Analysis of Murder" based on entirely reliable sources, although, objective and coldly unemotional as it was, it gave little comfort to our hangmen. This "Analysis" with my own researches, past and recent, have enabled me to draw up a simple Anatomy of English murders, with special reference to our own time.

A GENERAL PICTURE AND THE DILEMMA

The majority of England's murders are like the majority of murders in any advanced modern community for which statistics are available. Murders, on the whole, spring from sudden and momentarily ungovernable, passionate impulses. Hardly any of them are cold, premeditated, or planned crimes. About 25% of murders are motivated by mental disorder of some kind. Nearly 50% of murders occur concomitantly with quarrels, brawls, or fights, when tempers run high; or during phases of desperation or depression. Behind 1 in 25 murders there may be a revenge motive, or intrigue of some sort. 1 murder in 20 is associated with some sex activity (which, in Puritan England, usually makes for newspaper headlines). 1 murder in about 14 accompanies robbery. Other murders occur when avoiding arrest, or by accident, or for one or other of a variety of reasons which do not add greatly to incidence. You may ask what kind of general picture emerges from these cold figures? To me it is this: firstly, that the dominating colour is one of a mental instability (which may be momentary or chronic) that is always accountable for lack of balance or lack of control. Secondly, that the remaining colours are for the most part fairly evenly balanced. Thirdly, that all represent human weaknesses of consistently recurring patterns, which vary slightly in modern civilized communities and can often be traced to the strains and stresses of contemporary life. To the statesman the question is posed: what is to be done about murders in general? Can murderers, and the weaknesses nearly always found in them, be cured? Cured? Murderers can certainly be cured in a way which most certainly will prevent individuals perpetrating a second murder: by hanging. The deterrence of potential murderers in general is quite another matter. We look again at the statistics which show that during this century (up to 1959) the annual number of murders averages 3.8 per million of our population, and this *irrespective of hanging or not hanging or less hanging*—for we have had all three! Therefore, we can safely say that at all events hanging as a deterrent may be ruled out; unless our statesmen were to accept it as a useful and certain deterrent among the guilty by hanging murderers one and all. This might be unpopular to the point of losing votes, so no politician could agree to it; even last-ditch High Court hanging Judges, even the considerable body of hangers among the Lords Spiritual and Temporal might find all-out hanging a very awkward proposition. Hence a political dilemma, and we come back again to compromise, to the necessity for the expediency that is so useful in dealing with such political dilemmas as to hang or not to hang. The for and against campaigns will always find supporters, as in the past. The pro-hanging part of the public can take comfort that, so long as there is compromise, our hangmen will be able to keep their hands in; and that Home Secretaries will see that the gallows is kept oiled. Should the ropemakers lose their skill, one may look forward to the use of plastic ropes and possibly a mechanized gallows which, in our age of Science and artificial products, may break necks quite efficiently. Yet such hanging will never be the same as it was in the rich past, when fine craftsmen and artists made and did everything by hand.

HOUSE OF LORDS A SURE PREVENTIVE OF ABOLITION

The dilemma explains why it is that, although a Conservative government in 1959 had willy-nilly to shorten the hangman's rope, they could not entirely do away with it: the administration of criminal law of Britain is too dependent on party politics. A Labour Opposition would abolish capital punishment and indeed voted for its abolition in 1956, but the House of Lords, always vigilant and reliable about hanging, voted against abolition by 238 to 95. The House of Lords has proved itself to be a valuable barricade against all kinds of so-called progressive measures, including the abolition of capital punishment, a subject which seldom fails to warm up the emotions of the top English. The Upper House is a strange old institution, not without primitive urges of its own. On the occasion of the 1956 vote the "backwoodsmen"—those peers who so rarely put in an appearance in the House of Lords—turned up in fine fettle to vote against the threatening encroachments on England's freedom to hang. Men who had never stirred a muscle to put in an appearance on what one might think were matters of greater public interest were punctually on parade for the event: this rare gathering symbolized for England the last weight of feudalism in legislative power. As *The New Statesman and Nation* aptly put it at the time: "From the hills and forests of darkest Britain they came: the halt, the lame, the deaf, the obscure, the senile and the forgotten—the hereditary peers of England united in their determination to use their medieval powers to retain a medieval institution." It would be about as sensible to expect the House of Lords to abolish itself as to vote in favour of the abolition of capital punishment. One cannot see it ever doing either. The abolitionists, it seems, must first succeed in abolishing the medievalism of England's Second Chamber before they can hope to succeed in abolishing the hangman's rope. One has to take a long-term view of so deeply rooted an institution as the gallows. The English hereditary peerage regards all arguments against hanging as intolerable blasphemy.

A History of the Anti-Hanging Crusade

What has been said above should give heart to the pro-hanging element in English life. Abolitionists must always be patient people. There is a long history of patience behind them, as one may read in an excellent book, *The Crusade against Capital Punishment in England*, by an American author, Dr. Elizabeth Orman Tuttle

(Stevens, London 1961). Dr. Tuttle's book is a fine piece of research which must be studied to be fully appreciated. She has rendered a public service and, as history, her book is more valuable than any other on the subject. The anti-hanging crusade opened at least one hundred and fifty years ago, and continues as these lines are written. It has never fully succeeded, because, in addition to other reasons given in the pages of this modest Handbook, what is now called The Establishment in England has always been and, so far as one can judge, will always be against abolition. Civil Servants can be cold-blooded in secret if humane in public. If Dr. Tuttle's book points a moral, it is also a tribute to governmental obstinacy, *and* provides our hangmen with sound historical reasons to feel sure of their jobs.

CAPITAL PUNISHMENT *ABOLISHED*!

The year 1950, being that which marked the half-way stage in this twentieth century, is a good one with which to record the general opinion of the world on the question of capital punishment. Legal execution for the civil crime of murder had been abolished or allowed to fall into abeyance by a policy of reprieve in the following countries:

EUROPE: *Austria, Belgium, Denmark, Finland, Holland, Iceland, Italy, Luxemburg, Norway, Portugal, Romania, Sweden, Switzerland, U.S.S.R., Western Germany.*

In 1952 a campaign to reintroduce the death penalty in Western Germany culminated with the rejection by the Bonn Parliament of a Bill to reestablish the old practice. This happened on 31st October, and it was the second rejection of the death penalty by the Bonn Parliament. The campaign for reintroduction of the penalty was active in 1960–61.

AMERICA: Abolished in *Maine, Michigan, Minnesota, Wisconsin.*

Abolished also in *Rhode Island* and *North Dakota*—except for 1st degree murder committed while serving sentence for 1st degree murder. Also abolished in *Argentina, Brazil, Colombia, Costa Rica, Dominican Republic, Ecuador, Honduras, Mexico, Panama, Peru, Uruguay, Venezuela.*

ELSEWHERE: Abolished in *Queensland*. Also abolished in *New Zealand*.

Abolished in *Nepal* and *Travancore* in India.

During the Fascist régime in Italy, Mussolini reintroduced execution for crimes against the State and his own person. In 1950 the U.S.S.R. restored capital punishment for some political crimes, and so also did Peru in 1949. *Apart from these, the general world tendency in mid-twentieth century favoured abolition.*

Students of capital punishment—and all who think of such matters—often ask the question: What happens after the abolition of the death penalty? The more thoughtful may ask: How does the position after abolition compare with that before? I fear that what I am about to say may offend many of my retentionist friends—it may even hurt the feelings of our hangmen—but it must be said:

NO INCREASE IN THE NUMBER OF MURDERS AFTER ABOLITION

I am fortunately able to provide a useful summary, showing the position in those countries where the government has kept a statistical record of the position before and after abolition, though one must hope that the abolitionists will not flaunt these figures too flamboyantly under the noses of the retentionists. For all who have the interests of hanging at heart, much of this information is dynamite, but honesty demands that it be included here:

	Rate per
	100,000

HOLLAND. Death penalty abolished 1870.

Murder rate for 20 years before abolition	.095
Murder rate for 20 years after abolition	.093
Murder rate for 10 pre-war years 1931–40	.057

DENMARK. Death penalty abolished 1930.

Murder rate for period before abolition 1901–30	0.40
Murder rate for period 1931–40	0.23

NORWAY. Last execution 1875. Death penalty abolished 1905.

Murder rate before total abolition 1875–1904	.122
Murder rate after abolition 1905–24	.060
Murder rate for 10 pre-war years 1930–39	.036

(The last figure includes also manslaughter.)

SWEDEN. Death penalty abolished 1921.

Murder rate 15 years before abolition 1906–20	.049
Murder rate 15 years after abolition 1921–35	.058

SWITZERLAND. Death penalty abolished in 1942.

Murder rate in three years before abolition	.237
Murder rate in three years after abolition	.163

UNITED STATES OF AMERICA. Homicide rates for 10 years 1931–40 in the six States which abolished the death penalty:

Maine	1.70
Minnesota	2.35
Rhode Island	1.65
Michigan	4.35
North Dakota	1.75
Wisconsin	2.05
Average for the six abolitionist States for the 10 years:	2.3
Average for the whole of United States forthe 10 years:	8.1

But NOTE: the percentage of murders cleared up by conviction in the six abolitionist States in five years' period was 75.2, whereas for the whole of the U.S.A. only 63% of murders were so cleared.

ENGLAND AND WALES

See the statistics on page 59, and the commentary. While capital punishment was in abeyance in 1956–57, there was no increase in the murder rate. Nor was there a decline in this rate when hanging was reintroduced.

NOTE: The murder rate in England does not reflect fluctuations in the rate for crime in general. Murder must be regarded as a crime apart from other crimes.

In fairness to the reader it should be stated that the example of U.S.A. teaches the world little that is useful in regard to the abolition of the death penalty. Crime is endemic there, mainly because of a moral code which teaches that acquisitiveness and greed are the greatest desiderata in life. Money is held to be above all else; and, hence, men will do anything for it, as Christian missionaries do for their faith. The thief will commit murder for money, and, with its aid, feels almost certain to go his way unmolested. The "apprehension" of a murderer is regarded in the same light as a thunderbolt or an earthquake, namely, as an "Act of God." But in regard to *all* countries and States mentioned above, one solid truth emerges: the *abolition of the death penalty has not been followed by an increase in homicides.* Nor did the social order collapse, disintegrate, rot, or even shake with the departure from those States of what those who believe in State killing must regard as its key stone: the scaffold. After the vote for abolition on 14th April, 1948, in the House of Commons, hangings were suspended in Britain. *No increase in capital crimes followed*: a fact which confounded those who said that hanging was a deterrent. As recorded in this book, the House of Lords stood firmly by the hangmen, who were soon back on their jobs. But do not for a moment suppose that all this is likely to be used on behalf of the public as a powerful argument *against* hanging.

Not at all. The misguided peoples who no longer hang criminals little know what they miss and we really ought to do something to show them the error of their ways. It may even be argued that these black tracts of the earth's surface where the great salutary institution of the death penalty has been repealed by law, or left to grow mouldy with disuse, should be the object of a grand crusade. It would not be an easy crusade, because I fear that the only allies which England could find really in favour of hanging would be in the tattered remnants of her great Empire and certain equally high-minded States in the American Union.[12] From this the reader may conclude that hanging is now almost entirely an English practice. It is essentially English, in that it contains a sporting element which I have already illustrated by quoting the case of John Lee.

English Hanging "Done on the Sly"

When we look at this question in the cold light of reason, is it not disgraceful that the directly civilizing and humanizing influence of hanging should be limited to the sheriffs of England, the prison officials, and the clergy?—men who do not really require it. Public imagination in England is so limited that it does not reap the full benefit of hangings. This defect, coupled with the official strangulation at birth of all information on the subject, has caused hanging to become an almost useless institution when it should be salutary. Every good judge will agree with the logic of the Roman Catholic Bishop of Leeds, who, in reply to Mr. Josiah Oldfield's written question, "Do you suggest any alternative for hanging a murderer in semi-secrecy?" wrote, "*I should hang him publicly.*"

Why Not Hang in Public?

With regard to the actual hanging process, this could be made extremely impressive if executions were held in public. To do full justice to the ceremony, it would be necessary to employ a good impresario, and then the State could reap considerable financial benefits from public executions (to the financial and economic aspects of the question I shall return later). There are around London many admirable open spaces suitable for the execution of criminals. Shambles could be appointed in convenient parts of the metropolis, say in Hyde Park, Regent's Park, Trafalgar Square, and on the Horse Guards Parade for the special convenience of Members of the Cabinet and their families, who from rooms in No. 10 Downing Street, the Foreign Office, the Treasury, etc., would be provided with a good view and be able to contemplate the hangman at work in reality and not in imagination. Binoculars would bring it all closer. Spectators would realize that the hangman's work is not all beer and skittles, and they would see their representative as a very worthy being, a great patriot, and a man of true virtue, acting in *their* name and fulfilling an unpleasant task in an estimable manner. They do not at present fully realize the virtue and quality of his act.

MAKE HANGINGS MORE IMPRESSIVE

The massed bands of the Brigade of Guards could discourse sweet music, and a high Church dignitary, or his deputy on less important occasions, could preach a sermon based upon the text, "*An eye for an eye; a tooth for a tooth,*" or they could vary this with, "*Who so sheddeth man's blood, by man shall his blood be shed; for in the image of God made He man.*" Here I might interject that, although it is not generally publicized, both the hangman and the criminal are also made in the image of God. The pipers of the Scots Guards could no doubt add to the sermon a suitable lament, for the benefit of the assembled populace. There could not possibly be music more suitable for a hanging than that of the bagpipes. The Prime Minister would be able to watch the hangman put the finishing touches to his client, see him pause to make sure that all is ready; the pull of the lever, the sudden fall, the crack of doom and the last paroxysms of the body. The jury who found the prisoner guilty could afterwards file up to shake hands with the executioner, and congratulate him upon his proficiency. A special gallery conveniently situated should be provided for the British Medical Association, and the Council should be present with stop-watches. As a final wind-up, the Archbishop of Canterbury or his deputy should say the Lord's Prayer, emphasizing the words, "*Thy Will be done on earth as it is in Heaven.*" By way of further variety, an eminent theologian of modernist brand should make a speech showing that Christ was mistaken in His whole idea of redemption; that the Sermon on the Mount does not stand the test of higher criticism or anything equally relevant that comes into his head.

DECLINE IN HANGING

The world scarcely realizes that Britain is one of the most law-abiding countries in the world, mainly because bygone generations of Englishmen have insisted upon hanging the malefactor. Not very long ago hanging was extremely popular. A hundred and sixty years ago there were 200 offences for which a man, woman or child could be hanged. One could be hanged for cutting down a tree or for associating with gypsies: but, very strangely, not for associating with politicians. In the year 1832 it was abolished for stealing horses, sheep or cattle. In 1834 for "returning too soon from transportation." In 1835 for housebreaking, forgery, and inflicting bodily harm dangerous to life with intent to murder. In 1841 for abusing children under ten years of age. In 1861 for arson of dwelling-houses. Sir Robert Peel was one of those execrable men who have been responsible for this steady fall in popularity of the death penalty. Indeed, there are at present only four crimes in the English criminal law which are punishable with death: High Treason; Murder; Piracy with violence; Incendiarism in State dockyards. Three of these crimes are practically obsolete, and so there is really only murder for which punishment of death is inflicted. If further restrictions are placed upon the practice of the art, we shall soon not know how to hang pork, or even pictures.

INCREASE IN LAW: DECREASE IN VIRTUE

This decline in the popularity of hanging has been ascribed to "advances" in our civilization and social conditions generally. If we are to believe such trustworthy historians as the late Hilaire Belloc and G.K. Chesterton, we have not really progressed; and it would be an admirable thing for us to return to the rich, God-fearing, and spacious conditions of the Middle Ages. Every hangman will agree with this. But the question is: Is the decline in hanging due to decadence or to progress? That is a difficult question to answer, but, as there are so many signs around us of decadence, and few of any but technical progress, it is more reasonable for us to attribute it to decadence. We may assume it to be decadence. One thing is certain: it is bad financially and morally for our hangmen. They have little practice nowadays in their art more's the pity, and the sooner our legislators draw up a supplementary list of offences punishable by death the better it will be for our public safety and ultimate salvation. It would not be difficult to suggest such a list, but I do not propose to waste valuable space on it, however useful it might prove to the right kind of government. Yet there is one offence which must not be overlooked: the causing of mental anguish in any form to one's fellow man or woman. There ought to be a very simple code with the death penalty as a punishment for all sorts of offences that are now either completely ignored or very lightly treated by law. Highly complex law such as that which existed in Greece in the time of Solon, in Rome in the time of Justinian, and in England since the time of Birkenhead is indicative of decadence—though neither Greece nor Rome had laws comparable in sheer stupidity with Britain's laws relating to the sale of alcohol and for divorce. We have been frightened into law-abidingness without a corresponding increase in virtue. Virtue, true virtue, has suffered at the expense of a complex legal formalism. Women in this twentieth century have grown cold, calculating, and hard; in the happy Middle Ages they were frequently boiled "to soften their nature." It is, however, a matter of great contentment to all who have hanging seriously at heart that, after a sad lapse of seventeen years in England, there was a return to the practice of hanging women for the capital offence. Canada also (in May of 1924), after a lapse of twenty-four years, reintroduced the same practice. Thus the horizon of hanging is not without its bright spots, and, in spite of a very considerable movement for its abolition (by a class of person fatuously described as "humanitarian"), we may yet see some future development in the art. We can surely afford to thumb noses at "Humane Education" societies in this age of nuclear bombs and other products of our humanist science.

Vested Interests in Hanging

I often wonder if these abolitionists fully realize what they are up to, and that in this commercial and financial age they are endangering the bank balances of a whole host of people who are directly interested in hanging from a purely material point of view. Hangmen would be ruined by the success of their highly sentimentalized movement. Hemp-pickers, rope-manufacturers, carpenters, painters, bolt-makers, the makers of eyelets for the hangman's rope, printers who print the Book of Common Prayer used for the Burial Service of condemned men, lime merchants who provide the lime in which hanged convicts are often buried, and a host of others too numerous to mention would suffer financial losses if hanging were abolished in this realm. It is necessary to emphasize this grave commercial danger, and I trust sincerely that such bodies as the Federation of British Industries will do something about it, and Bankers' Bulletins, Trade Journals, and other publications read by the commercial world will give it full consideration: they are much more competent to do so than the present modest compiler. I have already discussed this aspect of the question with an eminent banker who is also interested in the daily Press; he immediately saw the point. He promised me that reviews of this book would be entirely favourable in all the newspapers he helps to control—and precisely because of this commercial danger. He entirely agreed with me that, apart from finance, hanging is necessary on moral grounds; and he epigrammatized the whole question by saying, "An irrevocable injury requires an irrevocable punishment." Or, in terms of mathematics: $1 + 1 = 0$. Thus his conscience justified his action with the newspapers. The preachings of humanitarianism, like those of Christianity, tend to cloud the public reason; and there is great danger that a sentimental government consisting of so-called humane men may be tempted to give way before the clamour of the mob in favour of abolishing capital punishment. The great British public was reassured by a statement made by the Home Secretary on the occasion of a gigantic petition for mercy for a condemned man. According to the *Times* report, the then Home Secretary[13]

> wanted to speak carefully, not too strongly, but sufficiently strongly to explain to the people of England that no Secretary of State worthy of his name could permit himself to be influenced in a matter of that kind by public clamour. Mob mercy was as bad as mob execution. We had heard of lynch-law in some parts of the world, and we considered it the most serious thing that could possibly happen in a civilized country. There was no difference between that and the attempts of a mob of 1,000 or 10,000 or 100,000 men and women to usurp the office of the Minister whose duty it was to deal with those terrible cases.

Mercy a Dangerous Thing

I should have thought there was a difference. Most men would rather receive a letter with 100,000 signatures than be hanged by a mad mob. But, as the Home Secretary nevertheless made clear, these petitions of mercy are in the long run not in the best interests of hanging, and the Secretary of State was quite right to discourage them. Mercy, and especially *mass* mercy, is a thing to be despised and suppressed by us all. If the spirit of mercy, indicated by the gigantic mass-petition mentioned, should continue at the rate at which it has grown of recent years, there is no saying where it may end. We might even see the abolition of war. What a disaster that would be! Imagine a world in which the spirit of Christ predominated, and human life was held to be sacred. Think of everyone, including the leaders of the innumerable sects of Christianity, living up to Christ's commandment, "*Thou shall not kill*"! Why, it is unthinkable! In some parts of the world, in mid-twentieth century—they were notable areas never yet directly touched by modern warfare—such was the feeling provoked by propaganda in favour of war that whoever preached peace was regarded as a political suspect, a dangerous "subversive" or just a plain lunatic. This sort of sentiment must not be permitted to take root anywhere. We must not forget that, although this mass mercy is not yet strong in England, out of seemingly unimportant happenings great movements have grown. A London fop once threw a coin to a lad for holding his horse outside the London Players' Theatre. Stung by the patronizing manner of the gift, the lad decided to do better things. He wrote *Hamlet*.

So away with all sentimental tosh, and let us get on with the hanging.

CONSULT THE HANGMAN

As long as we have politicians with a world-soul and universal conscience; men who are without passion or prejudices, who have the interests of the hangman at heart, men who are prepared to make personal sacrifices for the principles in which they believe, men who are humane: so long as we have these, the possibility of a reprieve need not cause sleepless nights to our public executioners. Notwithstanding all this, it would be well, in the interests of Justice, if the responsible Ministers made a practice of consulting the hangman in every case that comes before them for consideration of a reprieve. They need not necessarily be bound to follow the advice received.

DEAD MEN TELL NO TALES

We may usefully discredit the possibility of an innocent man being hanged, although before the Royal Commission of 1864 that inquired into the whole subject of Capital Punishment, the late Chief Baron Kelly gave evidence that in the course of some forty years there were twenty-two persons sentenced to death who were afterwards proved to have been innocent of the crimes for which they were sentenced. It is regrettable that such proofs should be given such publicity. They are bad for the honour of hanging. Besides, it is bad for a State and for authority that infallibility be demonstrated to be fallibility when an irrevocable punishment is carried out—one in which the innocent suffer and the guilty go free. Other cases could be cited of innocent men executed, though the official and correct view is "out of sight, out of mind," and "dead men tell no tales." In the Official Report of Debates in Parliament for 1881 will be found an account of a boy executed at Winchester. The prison chaplain rushed to London bearing a written confession made by a man for the very crime in question. This man was waiting to be hanged on another count. Even in those days Ministers went on holiday at awkward moments—just as they often do now. The chaplain could not find the Home Secretary in time; and so the poor boy was hanged. There is the much more spectacular and familiar case of Habron, who was found guilty of murder and afterwards proved innocent by the confession of the late Mr. Charles Peace, before he passed away. In the "Thorne" murder trial in 1925 the evidence of *three* expert witnesses, including that of Dr. R.M. Brontë—one of the most experienced pathologists then living—was to the effect that the way in which the death of Elsie Cameron took place, as alleged by the prosecution, was *impossible*. Yet the jury decided on the evidence of Dr. Bernard Spilsbury, official expert witness, that *probabilities* were of more cogency than impossibilities. On this decision Thorne was hanged. To this day the legal profession is divided in opinion as to his guilt. Not so the pathologists. Spilsbury's evidence has *since* been shown to have been very weak.

Chance of Errors Reduced to a *Minimum*

The Thorne case disturbed the hangmen of England because they were aware that the hanging of a possibly innocent man is thoroughly bad for the good name of their vocation. Hangmen are not the only citizens to be disturbed. In the Year of Grace 1951 the distinguished English peer Viscount Templewood, formerly Sir Samuel Hoare, a life-long Conservative, published a small book stating the case against capital punishment. The title of this book is *The Shadow of the Gallows*, and its importance lies chiefly in the fact that this true-blue Tory, a staunch supporter of Queen, Lords, and Commons and of Law and Order, of Church and State, of everything solid and stolid in Britain, and no doubt elsewhere, was Home Secretary in the years 1937–39. In other words he held the highly important post on which devolves responsibility for recommending mercy and reprieve for men condemned by a Court of Law to be hanged by the neck until dead. Lord Templewood all his life was a humane man. While he held power he did not shirk his grave responsibility, and when he deemed it necessary sent condemned men to the gallows. But, when he relinquished the ropes of power, he could safely allow conscience to get the better of him: with the result that he wrote this well-meaning little treatise against the State killing of murderers and against the noble art of hanging in particular. It was a sad lapse on the part of a respected politician; and deplorable from the point of view of our patriotic hangmen, all of them good Conservatives. Viscount Templewood adds to the list of men hanged whose guilt is in doubt or who were innocent, and brings it up to date; though he does not exhaust it.

He quotes among others the case of Reginald Woolmington (1935), about which there was a legal battle. In the end Woolmington was hanged, though one jury had failed to agree about his guilt. Lord Templewood asks pertinently, "Can there not have been other cases in which the wrong direction of a judge has led to an innocent man's death?" He quotes the Thorne case and foreign cases of innocent men convicted of murder, and even mentions the United States of America, where it seems juries and courts have also on occasion been known to show signs of fallibility. But Lord Templewood is careful to point out: "The chance of errors of judgment has, I have no doubt, been reduced to a minimum. If I have described them, it is certainly not because I wish to throw doubt upon the British judicial system." He concludes: "*It cannot be denied that mistakes can still occur.*" Elsewhere he says what this writer said in the first edition of this book, but my lord's words are so much better that they must be quoted: "Hanging was so much a part of English life that it was considered little short of sacrilege to try to restrict or abolish it." Happily for hangmen, that is still the position to day. The bishops stand firmly by the gallows; the judges favour the rope; the police are on the side of the hangmen; and the humanitarians, vegetarians, cranks, and egg-heads are treated with the contempt which they deserve. Life goes on in a war-weakened Britain and, whether in the midst of either a belt-tightening austerity or in a time of "never had it so good," or in a world threatened with destruction, the English hangman proudly symbolizes the spirit of a great people unwilling to see abolished the constitutional art which they have perfected. As Lord Templewood notes: "The result ... of a century of debate has been to leave the death penalty much as it was in 1862." Is not this something to be proud of? A clear case of "Onward, Christian Soldiers."

Hanging a "Ritual Sacrifice"

English hanging is an ancient institution, not in essence dissimilar from what social anthropologists call "ritual sacrifice," which is as old as the hills. Our hanging represents and symbolizes many things. First of all, it is a fulfilment of established law. And with that it is a satisfaction of, or catharsis of public vengeance against the murderer. It is intended as an example, by way of deterrent, to other potential murderers (not a very effective one, it seems; for they keep on cropping up with the utmost regularity year in and year out). And then there is in it a scapegoat element. The person hanged can take the place of either of the goats which Old Testament Hebrews sacrificed on the Day of Atonement. There were two goats, the Bible reader will remember, one of which had the sins of Israel confessed on it by the high priest. This one was driven into the desert and somehow disposed of, often by being cast over a precipice (if there should happen to be one convenient). The other goat was ceremoniously killed as a sin-offering. Similarly a good hanging can be the cathartic ritual sacrifice of a victim who, on being hanged in accordance with the traditional ritual, carries with him into eternity the murderous potentialities in all of us, thus symbolizing a liberation from them. Hence its uplifting moral value to so many good people.

HANGING AND RITUALISM

Many of us have read of the "ritual murders" which take place to this day in darkest Africa. The ideas on which they are based are sometimes simpler but often far more subtle than those behind the usual ritual sacrifice. But we call them "ritual *murder*" because they are against the laws of the occupying power and its colonial administration: just as a hanging is called a lynching or lynch-murder when it is done without legal sanction, though it also is a sort of cathartic sacrifice providing a release for the pent-up feelings of a mob. It is interesting to contemplate the great resemblance and indeed close sociological relationship between some of our more sensational English hangings and ritual murder. This is a complex aspect of our subject which ought perhaps to be left to the social anthropologists, who are much better equipped to deal with it than is the present writer. Yet it cannot be entirely ignored here, for have we not a very modern instance to illustrate the strong element of a religious ritualism persisting as tradition in our great and ancient institution?

EXTRAORDINARY CASE OF DEREK BENTLEY

The case in question was that of Derek Bentley, who was hanged in Wandsworth Prison in the Year of Grace 1953 for the murder of a police officer who, curiously enough, was shot not by Bentley but by a boy named Christopher Craig. Bentley was, in fact, safely under arrest when Craig fired the fatal shot. But English law wisely regards an accomplice in murder as a principal; and there was no doubt that these two youngsters were engaged on a felonious expedition. So, naturally, they were both found guilty of murder, but the jury, having a conscience, recommended Bentley to mercy. Because of his too tender age—sixteen years— Craig could not decently be hanged, so he was sentenced to be detained during Her Majesty's pleasure. Bentley was sentenced to be hanged by the neck until dead. Clearly this was a case out of the ordinary. Between sentence and hanging there was much public feeling and deep misgivings about executing Bentley for what was at most "constructive" and not actual murder. Many people thought that the Home Secretary, Sir David Maxwell Fyfe, a good Conservative lawyer-politician, and very well known for his decent general outlook on life, could not but accept the jury's recommendation to mercy and pass it on to our gracious young Queen. He did nothing of the sort. The jury's recommendation remained as so many futile words. Nor did the expressed view of Lord Chief Justice Goddard—that Bentley's guilt was less than that of his co-defendant Craig—have any noticeable effect on the Home Secretary, who was left with the awful personal responsibility for what now amounted to a political decision, for he had also to satisfy police feelings. When it was announced that the sentence must be carried out, all sorts and conditions of people, including many Members of Parliament, set to and did their utmost to have the decision altered. Not until then was it discovered—greatly to the surprise of most people—that even the House of Commons[14] could not find a way to alter a decision which involved the Royal Prerogative. A motion for a notice of debate was ruled by the Speaker to be "wholly out of order"; he could not permit a debate on this vitally important subject to take place. For the first time in their lives Members of Parliament and the public had it strikingly brought home to them that the inflexibilities surrounding and guarding the Royal Prerogative were acting in a way to silence even the House of Commons—the elected representatives of the people!—when the matter was the important one of to hang or not to hang. A Member asked whether the House must wait until Bentley was dead before it was entitled to say that he should not die. This Member was Mr. S.S. Silverman (Labour, Nelson and Colne). His energetic and exhaustive efforts on that occasion to break what England's public hangmen regard as an important safeguard of the Constitution must have earned for him an exceptional mark in the black books of executioners everywhere. And there were other protests: for the rigidity that had been injected into the Prerogative, while surprising many, came as a deep shock to others who may have thought that in this liberal and democratic realm there could not be anything so tainted with authoritarian totalitarianism, and which, it seemed, was in this instance as unalterable as the laws of the Medes and Persians. It meant death—as one Member put it—for "a three-quarter-witted boy of nineteen for a murder he did not commit and which was committed fifteen minutes after he was arrested." The ritual of hanging had to be fulfilled, and the blood sacrifice took place at 9 a.m. on Wednesday morning 28th January, 1953. At that hour outside the prison the police had to disperse the unorthodox and the misguided heretics who had assembled to demonstrate their disbelief in this ritual hanging which so manifestly was closely akin to those ritual murders of the African jungles.

The Writing on the Wall

The ritual hanging (or, if you wish, ritual murder) of Derek Bentley touched the emotions of the people of Britain. It disturbed our hangmen, for nobody knows better than they how bad a thing it is to hang an innocent man: and Bentley did not do the deed. Good judges of feeling—for example, the famous newspaper columnist Mr. Hannen Swaffer, and the distinguished playwright Mr. Laurence Housman, author of *The Hangman*—hinted that this execution might well prove to be a blow against the death penalty. At the time of writing no Gallup Poll had been taken of opinion among hangmen and their assistants, among the Lords Spiritual and Temporal, or other supporters, in regard to this case; but one knew that even among them opinion was divided. Great sympathy was expressed for the Home Secretary, who had fulfilled a hideous duty. Bentley was dead, but his name was immortalized by his hanging. For it is one to make supporters of capital punishment tremble and blush with shame. Was it a case of a political blunder? Whatever else it might be, it was some sort of writing on the wall: that much is certain. Perhaps the most disquieting feature of the Bentley case is that, after the boy was hanged, his father could show a physician's report of an encephalograph record which indicated that Bentley had been suffering from a disease of the brain which affected his behaviour.

Party Politics and Hanging

There can be no justice for the hanged when injustice is codified in law. The codification depends largely on Party Politics in England as in the Commonwealth and often elsewhere. I have this letter from an Australian author: "Did you know that in Australia it all depends on whether a Labour Government is in power (as now [1956] in Queensland) whether a man hangs or not? An Election is naturally of more than ordinary interest to a man found guilty there. At present [1956] you can be hung in South Australia, but not in New South Wales for an identical crime. In a year's time (after the Election) it may be the other way round ..." The writer adds: "Your book should be adult reading for every Member of Parliament and every adult with a vote. This would exclude our aborigines and half-castes, though they have some equal rights with white men: to fight for and be hung by their Government." Is it not touching how governments so often grant these two rights even to people of whom they may not think too highly?

MORE MISTAKES OF HANGMEN

Earlier in this book I have given instances of slight or chance errors of judgment (or, as some will have it, mistakes) on the part of hangmen, and looking through the immortal *Hansard* and elsewhere, I find a few more cases which are too important to be missed.

For example, when the famous Captain Kidd was hanged at Wapping on 23rd May, 1701, the rope broke not just once but *twice*. Some carelessness there! Then there is the more recent case of Mathew Atkinson, a mere pitman, who took a couple of drops in the city of Durham. *Hansard* tells the story thus: From the moment Atkinson was sentenced to death, he diligently applied himself to preparation for the happy life to come after the hangman had finished with him. At the ceremony, when the drop fell there was a rattle, a crash, a "horrible" thud, and the criminal had disappeared, and from the gallows was seen the broken end of a rope dangling in the wind! The half-strangled man, conscious of all that had taken place, was below the drop, bound hand and foot, his jaw, to use a euphuism, "horribly wrenched." Twenty-four minutes elapsed before the readjustments were made; and the official Parliamentary Report concludes, "The second hanging was successful." That was unpleasant enough, but there is on record the case of Brownless, whose bad life was not too well ended by the late Mr. Hangman Marwood. This also happened at Durham, and is reported in the ever-reliable Official Report of Parliamentary Debates known as *Hansard*. The great ceremony was, so it appears, very badly bungled and, when completed, it presented to the onlooker a spectacle so utterly "gruesome and revolting" that all intelligent advocates of the hangman's art trembled for its future. An onlooker reported:

> On looking down into the pit where the body hung we observed that the feet were about within half an inch off the ground; the rope, which was about an inch and a half thick, was embedded in the neck; and blood was slowly trickling down the breast.

And so on, in words unfit for an educational book such as this; and a grave reflection on the hangman.

Fun for the Hangman

Hansard gives also the case of a criminal called Connor. Another bad or, as enemies of the hangman say, bungled job. In this case the rope slipped. Connor turned to the hangman and, before the second attempt was begun, he asked with characteristic Irish impertinence, "What do you call this? Murder?"

Alas! Poor misguided Connor! Did he not see that it was merely one of those slight miscalculations common in all spheres of life? Then there was the case of Johnson, hanged by the late Mr. Hangman Askern at Leeds. The rope broke. The contractors who supplied this rope were doubtless to blame; and it would be unjust to attribute the fault, if any, to the hangman. The public are far too quick to blame the unfortunate hangman, who, in most cases, does his work conscientiously, and on occasion is even complimented by the condemned man, before the final drop is taken. This happened of a man called Rowles, at Oxford; which, even so late as 1878, was still a focus-point of *Literae Humaniores*. The influence of humane letters was distinctly felt on this occasion: the criminal extolled his own death; and actually kissed the rope. At the trial the jury had strongly recommended him to mercy, saying that he had been "tempted by the devil," which no doubt he was. He was duly hanged in the best Oxford manner.

ALWAYS HANG WOMEN

It is not very long ago since it was alleged in Parliament that pregnant women were carefully nursed in prison until the time when, after having given birth to a child ... they could be handed over to the hangman. We now live in a more sentimental age, and, although this is still permissible by law, it is simply not done. It will be obvious even to the most innocent reader that not to hang pregnant women may be one way of encouraging sexual misconduct as a means to escape the gallows. Is it not ridiculous and immoral that a woman who has committed murder should escape the death penalty by amusing herself with the first man she meets? There is on record the case of a pregnant woman who procured an abortion, and after that event was arrested on a murder charge. She was found guilty and duly hanged; had she not procured the abortion, she would be alive today. All this must be changed. If a woman is found guilty of murder she must be hanged, pregnant or not pregnant, abortion or no abortion—and there's an end to it. As I have hinted before, we must away with sentiment, for it is universally recognized that, of all animals, woman is the most dangerous. Why, as recently as February 1951 a woman in New Zealand had the impertinence to apply for the post of public executioner. A hang-woman! Now if women are willing to hang men, why need men be squeamish about hanging women? Perhaps it is because men are better sports.

Here I should like to display my erudition on a point not irrelevant to what may be termed the "Inhibitions" of hanging. In the third book of his *Essays*, Montaigne (although he refers somewhat slightingly to the office of executioner) opens up a new vista for hangmen in the story he relates of the daughter of Sejanus, who could not (by a certain provision of Roman Law), be punished with death because she was a virgin. In order to allow the law to take its course, she was violated by the hangman before being strangled. Montaigne comments:

> Not only his hand, but his soul is a slave to public convenience.

He then refers to the hangman as worse off than the hanged. Some may not believe him in regard to this. It depends on the type of woman. The sentimentalist is the curse of all good cause and, when we consider this question of hanging, he enters into it like the crank who favours nature healing as against surgical operations.

Although we do not now keep women in prison until they have given birth to a child, and then calmly turn them over to the hangman, it is interesting and educative for us to contemplate what happens to an accused man who in an affray has committed a murder and has not done it without damage to his own person. Such a man is nursed back to good health and condition with all the tenderness which a benevolent government can place at his disposal, in order that he may be hale and hearty for the drop. I shall state an imaginary case to illustrate my point. One day it may be used as a contribution to a certain magazine, to which I shall refer later.

ROMANCE IN A BUTCHER'S SHOP

This romance (let us imagine) happened in a butcher's shop, and may be worthy of mention as an example of the elevation to which human sublimity can rise. The facts are simple—idyllic in their simplicity—and I think not without a touch of poetry. The *dramatis personae* are a butcher, his assistant, and the butcher's wife. The butcher is a kindly, good-natured man, and his wife equally pleasant. But let us continue in the past tense: she was much younger than he; and the customers all spoke well of her sweet smile and generous nature. These significant facts were not lost upon the assistant, who was somewhat of a ladykiller, metaphorically speaking. He began to cast sheep's eyes (metaphorically) at the handsome wife of his employer; and his amorous advances were not unwelcome. The situation is not without parallel. A triangle—an isosceles triangle—was formed, in which the base was the wife and the sides were the butcher and his assistant.

A Hypothetical Murder

One morning in Spring, when a young man's heart turns to love, a middle-aged man's to jealousy, and an old man's to regrets, the butcher caught his assistant in the cash-desk discussing the quality of mutton with his wife. Looking about the shop for some suitable tool with which to punish the young man's presumption, the butcher picked up a meat-chopper made of good Sheffield steel. He swung it dexterously, as indeed might be expected, but the assistant quite intelligently observed what was happening, and dodged cleverly. He received the mere edge of the blow, so to speak, upon his occiput. Stung to action, he drew from his belt a long, sharp knife with which he had been accustomed to slice chops, liver, and steaks; and without a moment's hesitation he drew it cleanly across the butcher's throat. The butcher withdrew to collect his breath.

Meanwhile the wife constituted herself a referee.

The End of a Dream

A few moments later the butcher recovered and prepared to resume the fight. Raising the chopper above his head, he steadied himself, balancing upon the flat of his feet, and took scientific aim at his assistant's head. He brought the chopper down with such force and accuracy of aim that he thought the combat was over. But the assistant, by a supreme effort of will, got up and drew his knife (this time transversely) across the jugular vein of his opponent.

Both men fell to the ground, and the butcher's wife called time in a loud voice. The assistant was silent for ever. He died fighting for his love, in memorable combat. To pass over quickly the pulsating romance of this story, and to come to that part of it which bears directly upon the subject of the present treatise, the butcher is "apprehended" for his "altercation." He is duly charged with murder; they place him in the ward of a prison hospital and he is given the best treatment of which modern medical science is capable. In time, his neck heals and, by the Grace of God, he fully recovers his health and spirits. He becomes *mens sana in corpore sano*, and ready for trial. During his sojourn in hospital he is given attention other than medical. A full statement, amounting to a confession, is taken by the authorities. Upon this, the man is condemned to death. And they hang him.

Now, although I am not in favour of helping the escape of anybody who ought to help swell the hangman's exchequer, I am of the opinion that this sort of thing (for, although the case is hypothetical, it is just what might easily occur) illustrates a certain falling off in the sporting instincts of the English nation. Had such an incident occurred a few hundred years ago, the butcher, instead of being treated as a felon, would have become a popular hero. Furthermore, the fact that he had survived a mighty combat would be accepted as proof not merely of the justice of his cause, but of his innocence of evil intent. Now we nurse him round to life—merely in order that he may be hanged by the neck until such time as it may please the All-merciful to remove life from his quivering body.

POPULARITY OF MURDER TRIALS

It is a fact that present methods of trial tend to make a hero of the murderer, who, when he is condemned to death, completely overshadows the hangman in popularity. Of recent years there has been far too much sickly sentimentalism over criminal trials culminating in the perfectly legitimate hanging of the criminal.

The preliminaries, trial, period of rest in prison before execution, are exploited by an energetic Press. The reason for all this is that the criminal risks his life at the trial; and forfeits it if he is found guilty. The public loves to see a man risk his life: think of the excitement and fun in dirt-track racing (and motor racing generally), in trapeze acts at the music-hall, in crossing the road through traffic, in an operation on a very important person, in a bull-fight, in a steeple-jack's job, or what not. It seems unfair that such a spectacle as a murder trial should be restricted to the favoured few who can elbow their way into Court during a hearing.

Nothing is more interesting to the student of psychology than a really good murder trial. At the same time, the proceedings could and should be brightened considerably. The space set aside for the public is not enough. The Albert Hall, the Coliseum, or even the Stadium at Wembley (if equipped with loudspeakers and a good commentator) would be infinitely better for murder trials than our stuffy, uncomfortable Law Courts.

PLAN TO LOWER THE INCOME TAX

The Treasury could easily draw up a scale of charges for admission, and the money so raised could be set aside towards the provision of better remuneration and pensions for our gallant hangmen. I have no doubt but that, even allowing for generous treatment of executioners, there would still be a fair sum left over to alleviate our Income Tax, which strikes most of us as excessive. The fund could be further swelled by the sale of the film rights in the trial and execution of murderers and, as a sop to the public, the Entertainments Tax on admission charges to all such ceremonies could be waived, they being of educational value. A friend of mine (an unchartered accountant) in 1928 provided me with the following figures, showing how much the State could benefit if a murder trial and execution were conducted as they ought to be: the figures are pre-Second World War and would now be many times higher. Here they are:

I	Rent of Albert Hall per day	=	£200
	Salary and Pension Fund for,		
	say, one dozen hangmen	=	100
	Sale of seats per day	=	2,500
	Total daily profit	=	£2,200

II	Sale of Film-rights		
	(a) of one dozen good trials	=	£12,000
	(b) of one dozen good hangings	=	£3,000
		=	£15,000

These are British figures. In Hollywood they would probably *pay* much more, but it is doubtful if they could deal more sympathetically with the art of the hangman than the British. The Americans are often very brash and European critics have accused Hollywood of vulgarity, which in hanging would be intolerable.

The first total represents the net profit for one day. But 100 or more days are occupied in murder trials every year at the Central Criminal Court. So,

£2,200 x 100 = £220,000 *per annum*

Even allowing for inflation[15] a very useful sum of money is involved, but, apply the same financial principles to *all* the murder trials held throughout the country in the course of a year, and what is the result? Today a sum of not less than ten million pounds a year could find its way into the Exchequer. If the whole matter were put into the hands of a really competent impresario, I have no doubt but that the figure ultimately reached for a reduction of the Income Tax would be a very much higher one, and if a Chancellor will but use this idea, he may turn it to admirable account for his next Budget. In this manner a government might be preserved in power, a little money could be set aside towards the next war to end war, and all risks of the abolition of the death penalty removed. I am sending a copy of this book to our political offices, and I hope it will be of use at the next General Election.

I do not expect any reward for my suggestion, as a progressive I have at heart *only* the interests of the country.

HANGED FOR SHEER STUPIDITY

The death penalty is intended by the State to be a deterrent of murder. In proof that it does deter we have an average of about 150 murders a year in England. In the United States of America they have thousands. If, as some logicians believe, hanging is a deterrent of murder, why should Mr. Hangman John Price have been hanged for murder on 31st May, 1718? Incidentally, Mr. Hangman Dennis was hanged (*c.* 1780) for "helping to pull down a dwelling-house"! They apparently took their chances, like others or, knowing how nice hanging really is, they just courted it. If further proof were necessary that hanging need not deter, there is the story of the late Mr. Hespel, an executioner who deplorably let down his craft by turning murderer himself. One day (he was off duty at the time) he committed a really artistic piece of slaughter. With all his experience of hanging as a deterrent, one might have expected that he would never have committed such an offence, for, as we know, the death penalty deters and he himself had helped to inflict it on innumerable occasions. The least we can say is that he was a particularly stupid type of man, and a disgrace to the clean annals of execution. His act was, indeed, the Koh-i-noor of nonsense. It may be that for a moment he forgot himself and thought that he had in his pocket the permission of the law to kill, if so, his absentmindedness got him into serious trouble. A hangman has only a *temporary* license to kill—unlike doctors, the Royal Ulster Constabulary, drunken motorists, etc. Perhaps he thought that by murdering somebody he would prevent other people from acting similarly. So far as all my researches go, I have not been able to find that he deterred one potential murderer from murdering, with the possible exception of his victim on that occasion. He was duly executed for his stupidity. This sad case is rather like a *reductio ad absurdum*, but it must not on that account be advanced as an insidious argument against hanging. Honourable mention is due to the modern American hangman who flourished in Macalester, Oklahoma, until 1952, when he died from natural causes after a life of service in which he hanged sixty-six men. This was Mr. Rich Owens, whose place in hanging history is safe because of one thing: he was acquitted of murder on no less than four occasions! Hence, no man could be more suitable for the post.

When we look closely into it, there are two categories of people who commit murder: (1) Those who are sane (know the nature and quality or consequences of their act) but hope to escape the penalty; (2) Those who are insane, and these either do not know or do not care what they do. Homicides are either the one or the other, so it is difficult to appreciate the deterring effect of the death penalty upon their minds. I am not a psychologist or metaphysician, or even a theologian, so I cannot resolve this difficult problem except by saying that, if a man knows what will happen as a result of an act of his, and hopes so strongly to escape the consequences that he actually commits the act, a contemplation of the possible penalty does not seem to me to hinder him.

A BOOK AGAINST HANGING

Whether the death penalty deters or does not deter would-be murderers from committing murder is, when we sum it up, a matter of speculation. If anything, the evidence shows that it does not deter, and most of this evidence was given in E. Roy Calvert's pioneering work *Capital Punishment in the XXth Century*.[16] I really ought not to mention it, as it is a work which has derogated considerably from the great art with which this Handbook deals. But it is necessary that we should treat hanging as objectively as possible, and the reader need not peruse Mr. Calvert's book if he is not interested in that *other* and far less important side of the question.

Depressing Side of Hanging

Let us turn now to a depressing aspect of hanging, and consider a few of its immediate effects. Apart from the public there are certain persons directly concerned in the business: the person who is hanged; the hangman; and the prison staff. We all know the effect upon the person who is hanged. His neck is broken, or he is strangled; at all events he is killed, even if (as I have shown) the process is frequently long-drawn out. The effect upon the warders who surround the condemned man, and upon the hangman who does the job, is sometimes very disheartening for those who are in favour of a continuation of capital punishment. The strain of having to attend executions is sometimes more than even the most hardened warders can stand. In 1924 there was the case of the former chief warder at Wandsworth Prison—the late Mr. Lazell— who was so worried by his memories that he committed suicide, and even tried to reproduce a hang-house scene in so doing. It is bad enough in all conscience when a mere spectator will do this sort of thing, but it is really most depressing to find that there is a whole history of hangmen and other specialists in State execution who have, by one means or another, attempted to do away with themselves. And who have succeeded. Until fairly recently we had with us the ex-hangman Mr. John Ellis, who resigned his post in March 1924 after holding it honourably for twenty-five years, during which time he assisted or presided at some 200 executions, all of which were, in accordance with the Home Office instructions (not to divulge facts to the contrary), carried through with expedition.

A Famous Modern Hangman

Mr. Ellis was a man of towardly parts, homely manners, renowned for his proficiency and art. It is melancholy to have to record of such a man, of whom it has been written that he was too tender-hearted to wring the neck of one of his own fowls, that his experience in hanging the late Mrs. Thompson—who was carried unconscious from her cell to the hang-house—drove him to attempt to commit suicide. The account of it given in the Press[17] is this. Shortly after one o'clock in the morning his family were awakened by the noise of a revolver discharge, and poor Mr. Ellis was found lying on the floor of his living-room, bleeding from the neck. A revolver lay beside him. He was brought before the magistrates and charged with attempting to commit suicide. The Chairman asked him if he was prepared to give an undertaking that he would not again attempt suicide; and to this Mr. Ellis agreed. The Chairman of the Bench then replied in well-chosen words, as follows:

> I am sorry to see you here, Ellis. I have known you for a long time. If your aim had been as true as some of the drops you have given, it would have been a bad job for you. Your life has been given back to you, and I hope you will make good use of it, and lead a good life in atonement.

Very fine sentiments, too, except that the logic seems to be wrong; a life which has not been taken away can hardly be given back. Mr. Ellis said on this occasion that he had "some drink taken." One can understand why. Throughout his career he was forbidden to stay at public-houses, as his sojourn might "attract custom." Why not? Now a hangman has a thirst like other men, and it is quite conceivable that Mr. Ellis was enjoying the freedom of retirement, and had "one over the eight." There is an old saying *in vino veritas*, and this is an interesting case in human psychology, if human is the correct word.

THE GREAT HANGMAN INTERVIEWED

It was the very great privilege of this writer to make the personal acquaintance of the late Mr. Ellis, that great High Hangman of England, who in his day endeared himself to the public and was so much loved by candidates for the gallows that they would say, "I hope Ellis hangs me." It was at Great Yarmouth when in retirement he was giving his famous lecture on hanging with a demonstration of the working of a gallows and his own part in an execution. "You can't beat English hanging," this eminent hangman said to me, as we chatted on the beach one summer's day, while he allowed the grains of Yarmouth sand to trickle through his fingers as if to symbolize a gravitational flow of life towards death. Those other ways of putting away murderers— he always used the verb "to put away" never "to execute," and rarely "to hang"—were either mean or messy. Whenever he spoke of hanging he would run his tongue round his lower lip as if he could taste the flavour of it, and once he paused to look me up and down as if mentally taking my weight and measure for a drop. With a convincing finality, and pointing an index finger heavenwards, Mr. Ellis looked me straight in the neck and exclaimed: "Now, sir, hanging is *clean*. It's the cleanest way of all of putting them away. In fact it's English—as English as cricket or plum pudding, or Worcester Sauce." He was contemptuous of electrocution, which he said was a c-r-u-e-l business because the client was sometimes part cooked like a herring on a griddle. Terrible!—especially for "them present," that is. Ellis's chief anxiety seemed to be for "them present," and the man hanged was to him a mere abstraction who (or which) did not matter. "In hanging," said he, looking at me sideways with a smile like the Mona Lisa, "it's all over in a second or two before you could say Jack Robinson. No mess either—or very rarely. A touch of the lever and *squonk*, a few kicks and maybe wheezes and"—he snapped his fingers—"it's all over bar the inquest and collect the dough." To illustrate how expeditious it is, he laughingly told me an anecdote. A hangman on one occasion by mistake whipped the white cap over the prison chaplain's head, adjusted the rope and was about to give him the drop when suddenly—and only just in time—the parson's cassock was spotted. "Which just shows you!" he added, lighting a cigarette. Guillotining? Too messy! Asphyxiation? Ellis lowered his head, looked at me under his eyelids showing the whites of his eyes, and commented sadly that one day it might come to that. But asphyxiation is *too soft*; and useless as an example to the public. The public would "get no kick out of it" as they do from hanging. Imagine picking up a Sunday newspaper and reading that So-and-so, the murderer, had been put away by asphyxiation! Why, it would be as if somebody had passed out under an anaesthetic! And what use was that? Ellis warmed up: "It's the *good example* in it that makes British Governments stick to hanging," he said, "and they are wise. How could you make a better example of anybody than by hanging him?" I suggested drawing and quartering, to which he immediately replied: "Out of date. The humanitarians and the squeamish would object; and maybe even the bishops and judges would protest." Ellis was not averse to beheading with an axe, but "only for high-ups," as in the past. In a democracy hanging was best every time: especially when "done proper." As for him, he'd never bungled a hanging. All the same, women were a great nuisance. When they hanged Edith Thompson everybody present was upset to vomiting point. Hanging women upset most hangmen; and you just shouldn't do that. "We don't make mistakes nowadays," he assured me; "it's all taped and worked out, and even if there should be some slight mishap the whole government machine goes all out to save the hangman's face. *They have to*." Again he looked me straight in the neck and said, "No one ever had to save my face." I could well believe it. That fine High Hangman of England, the reader will be distressed to learn, has gone to the great beyond. But he has left a fragrant memory. We may leave him to deal with the problem which will face him on the other side if he should run into some of his earthly clients. It would hardly be surprising if some of those clients awaited his ascension (or descension, as the case may be). Here is an aspect of the subject deserving of contemplation, and it seems a great pity that, as on some other aspects of life after death, we are lacking in precise information. The theologians are no great help, even when they expand the boundaries of their own belief and ours.

Pride in Profession

An afterthought. Before we *finally* part from the good Ellis, I remember one strong impression I had at the time of the interview: Ellis's pride in his profession and his conceit in personal publicity relating to it. I asked him whether he kept notes of his executions and he said, "No need—I used to keep press-cuttings about them," on which I remarked, "You must have a very valuable collection." An expression of acute agony came over his cheerless features and he said mournfully: "*No!* It was like this. One evening, after a good session in a pub, I was sorting them out for an autobiography I intended to write. I was sitting at home by the fire at the time, and must have fallen asleep. For I woke up on the floor and saw the last flames of the very best of my fine collection dying out before my eyes. I don't mind telling you that I cried—yes *cried*. Just imagine! The record of a long career—gone up in flames!" Tears again trickled down his cheeks. I asked him whether the autobiography would ever be written and he said, "Although a Sunday paper made me a good offer, I just can't face it. I remembered *everything* by those cuttings, and now I feel so lost that I could never do the job justice." All I could say in the circumstances was that it would be a great loss to posterity and leave an irreplaceable gap in the national history: to which he nodded in solemn acquiescence. Ellis never gave up his belief in hanging, but he was no hypocrite about it. He did not believe in it as a deterrent but merely as retributive justice in the Old Testament sense. He was at heart a fundamentalist. *Vale Ellis. In omni labore emolumentum est.*

Love *Versus* Career

It is quite extraordinary the prejudice some people have against hangmen and their work for the State. An incident which happened in the Spring of that memorable year 1960 illustrates the fact. An Assistant Hangman had fallen in love with a sweet Spanish girl but she would not agree to marry him "Unless"—

to quote her own words—"you stop helping to hang people." The youth was the son of Harry Allen, Britain's new Hangman-in-chief, who succeeded the great Pierrepoint when the latter retired with his unblemished record. Harry keeps the Junction Inn, an excellent pub at Whitefield, near Manchester. "I'd been in two minds about quitting the job," said young Brian Allen, "but when Angela asked me to drop it, that decided me," he told the *Daily Sketch* (26/5/1960). And he did drop it, for it was a clear case of love of a woman triumphing over love of career. Brian concluded: "Of course, Dad and I don't talk about the hangman's job. I know it is supposed to run in families, but I've decided it is 'out' for me—though someone has to do it." His father made him manager of the pub and his beautiful bride wound up smiling: "And *we* won't talk about hanging." A happy ending to the story, even though a good man has been lost to the public service.

More Difficult to Hang one Woman than two Men!

I had almost omitted to mention that Mr. Hangman John Ellis had some business correspondence with a Sir John Samuel (an important official) in February 1922, in which he quoted his fees: "You can rely on me being at Glasgow on Tuesday morning ... My fees are £15 for each execution, first-class return railway fares and cab fares. In the event of a reprieve, half fees £7.10s." In Scotland, as in England, they hang women, when necessary. In 1923 they hanged a woman named Susan Newall. Of this Ellis wrote apropos: "*It is more difficult to execute a woman than two men*, and I propose that Mr. P. Baxter, of Hertford, goes with me as he was one of the assistants who was with me at Mrs. Thompson's execution ... Will you please ask the Prison Commissioners to send the special body straps made for Mrs. Thompson." You may remember that there was considerable public outcry about the hanging of Mrs. Thompson. It leaked out that this was altogether a rather horrible business, and Ellis himself did not like it because of the anguish it caused to the onlookers. He was not taking any risks with Susan Newall. Of the hanging of Mrs. Thompson Major Lloyd was able to assure the House of Commons that "in the case of Mrs. Thompson the proprieties were observed."[18]

But now to return to that depressing side of our subject, the suicides which occur from time to time in the ranks of the most excellent executioners.

A New Orientation in Capital Punishment

In the early months of the year 1926 a retired German headsman (*Scharfrichter*, from *scharf*—sharp, and *richter*—judge) shot himself at Breslau, and this suicide was immediately followed by that of his successor. Then there was the Australian executioner who carved his own throat rather than hang a woman; and under Alfonso XIII the Spanish official garotter drew his own precious life to a close. Even John Hulbert, a prosperous New York executioner, apparently committed suicide (1929). There was just then an epidemic of suicides amongst executioners; and for a moment it looked as though the whole question of capital punishment was taking what diplomats, with characteristic aptness, call "a new orientation." The case of old Herr Schweitz was undoubtedly caused by the fall in the mark. He had retired some fourteen years previously on a pension at a fixed rate, and inflation caused its value to dwindle to almost nothing. The grand old veteran—the Hindenburg of Headsmen—made a valiant attempt to supplement his mere pittance, first by writing a treatise on his speciality (it is a valuable contribution to contemporary science) and next by quixotic efforts to popularize decapitation, by lecturing upon it and by exhibiting the axe with which he had removed the most dangerous protuberance of a large number of criminals. But alas! the rise in the cost of living was so swift that, notwithstanding the literary success—it was more than a mere *succès d'estime*—of his efforts, and the undoubted popularity of his public appearances, the financial returns were disappointing. Faced with misery in his old age, there was only one course open to him; and he took it. Here is one more pathetic example of what may easily become a general practice if States neglect to reward fittingly the great public services of individuals. We must not condemn the German Government for their failure to smooth the old age of this patriot, when we ourselves make no adequate provision for the old age and decrepitude of our hangmen.

EXECUTIONERS ARE GOOD CHRISTIANS

The suicide of Herr Schweitz's successor was also foreshadowed by a series of untoward incidents. Herr Paul Spaethe (that was the gentleman's name), like so many executioners, was an extremely religious man. In time, with the practice of his science (yes, science and not art, as in the case of hanging) his religion grew more and more gloomy, until at last it became a sort of obsession. It is to the credit of this good Christian that (in common with most State killers) he never once permitted his religious scruples to interfere with his decapitations. Just before his own decease he struck off the head of a criminal at Cologne (or Köln, as the Germans persist in calling it). When he decided to commit suicide he prepared the way to depart this life by burning one candle for each head that he had severed during his short term of public office. Could anything be more sublime? Herr Spaethe is now in Heaven. With him is Herr Lang, the Austrian State executioner who, in the *Gleichshaltung* of 1938, committed suicide. It is necessary to pause and consider these very recent cases in order to see that, although these excellent patriots did actually commit suicide, it was not because of any jabs of conscience for having successfully performed their very important task of execution. In each case there were other circumstances which, if not the immediate cause of their suicide, at all events offered a strong contributory impulse towards it.

Digression on the Nazis

Speaking of Germany reminds the present writer of a little story which should now be regarded as a contribution to the folklore of Nazidom. Students of history will remember that the Weimar Republic abolished capital punishment. German headsmen went into retirement, but as Adolf Hitler and his friends gathered political momentum those headsmen began to regain hope. A philosopher of Italian Fascism had written that the capital punishment of those who were a danger to the State was an accepted tenet of that creed; and German National Socialism seemed unlikely not to accept so useful a principle. It so happened that a distinguished Englishman (who was interested in the rise of Hitler) used to visit Germany before the Führer came to power. One morning, in the early 1930s after a heavy political banquet, this Englishman decided to go out of the city for a walk in the open country—just to get a breath of fresh air and clear his head. As he walked across a field in the early morning mist he saw at some distance ahead the figure of a tall, well-built man who appeared to be chopping wood in a curious manner. On approaching him the Englishman noticed that it was not wood but turnips he was chopping; and that they were not being chopped into small pieces but were merely cut in two. The tall man, each time he cut a turnip, went through a ritual as follows. He would pick up a turnip from a heap, mark it, place it on a log, stand back, swing his formidable axe, bringing it down with a swish, and he nearly always cut the turnip neatly into two pieces. Then he would stand back, draw himself sharply to attention, raise his right hand in the Nazi salute, look solemnly skywards, and say aloud, "*Heil Hitler!*" Pause. And then he would repeat the whole ceremony over again. In this way he had reduced the heap of turnips until few remained to be dealt with. The Englishman was deeply interested, and in his best German asked the tall man what exactly he was doing. "Merely keeping my hand in," the tall man replied. When the Englishman showed by his face that he was puzzled, the tall man said: "Have you not heard the phrase '*Heads shall roll*'? Well, I advise you to study politics. I am a principal executioner and headsman. Decapitation is a certain cure for political dandruff. Mine is going to be a fine job soon, and I wish to be able to defy competition." With those words he took up a turnip, placed it on the block, and, with the words "*And heads shall roll*," cut it expertly in two with a swing of the axe, and repeated the words "*Heil Hitler*!" The headsman proved to be a prophet. Hitler, as we know, came into power. And the heads did roll in Nazi Germany, as we also know. But hanging and decapitation could not cope with the numbers of people who were not wanted by Hitler and his friends. After consultation among the best German scientists, new methods were evolved. With them the colourful old methods were replaced by the merely efficient and sordid.

GREAT ERA OF EXECUTION

What an Era of Execution that of the Nazis then became! Some two and a half million people were later executed at Auschwitz alone, by gassing and burning. This was the German official estimate offered in his solemn affidavit to the Nuremberg Tribunal by Rudolf Hoess, Commandant of the camp. "At Auschwitz," he said, "I used Zyklon-B, which was a crystallized prussic acid dropped into the death chamber. It took from three to fifteen minutes to kill the people in the chamber, according to climatic conditions. We knew when the people were dead, because their screaming stopped." Most unpleasant, according to our more decent English ideas. Yet one must not overlook the fact that the gas-chamber method of execution, as practiced by the Nazis, symbolizes the basic logic of capital punishment; and that Hitler's attitude of mind towards this, and other subjects of common interest to humanity, caters for thoughts and emotions which have an almost universal currency and are certainly not limited to Germans. How many excellent British people, whose names we all know, found arguments to justify, if not their open support for Hitler and Nazism, at least their sympathy for the great *Führer* and his acts? And if another Hitler were to arise, he would find similar supporters and sympathizers. Alas, poor humanity!

This digression and homily ended, we may now return to the cleanliness and main thread of our subject.

Royal Executioners and Aristocratic Hangmen

Yet before permitting ourselves full momentum I should like to remind those ignorant people who are often inclined to sniff and look down their noses at executioners in general and hangmen in particular that there have been some very distinguished members of royal families and of old aristocracy—and in more countries than one—who, throughout a long life of public sacrifice and service, also took upon themselves the office of public executioner and *personally* undertook the act of dispatching the undesirables. I shall quote only two here, as our space is valuable and we need it for the true professionals. The royal executioners did the work as a labour of love; and were attracted to it by its—attractiveness. Our first example is Peter the Great of Russia. Peter prided himself on his skill in beheading with the axe, and whenever there was a head, or heads, to be struck off, he would drop what he was doing or get out of a warm bed on a freezing cold Russian morning in order to satisfy his human yearnings. Most of his biographers tell us of this life-long habit of the first of the Romanovs. Stephen Graham writes of one important public function:[19] "And who was the tall heads-man leaning on his axe, this giant of the scaffold? It was not a sovereign seeking popularity. The executioner was Peter himself, who on the first day of the executions struck off two hundred heads with his own axe." Those were the days! As an axeman Peter was skilful, and until late in life rarely failed to sever a head with one stroke. Curiously enough the English were never first-rate headsmen—their hearts are really in hanging—and we read that even the great executioner chosen to dispatch the Earl of Essex had to have three goes before the head was severed, so that he could hold it up before the privileged spectators shouting,

"God save the Queen!" But enough of this bloody stuff, and back to clean hanging. In our own century it is on record that the late Franz Josef, Emperor of Austria and King of Hungary (1830–1916), of beloved memory, prided himself on his *expertise* in the fine art of hanging. But he did not publicize whatever work he may have done in this line, for he was a modest man and completely lacking in the *prostór*, the flamboyant Russian "spaciousness" of Peter the Great. Furthermore, Franz Josef lived in a hypocritical age when sentimentalism might have taken umbrage at royal personal participation in State killing. Royalty, as a rule and in accordance with royal dignity, merely nods a gracious approval. Hence, authentic details are lacking, more's the pity. As for aristocrats who have got a thrill from hanging their inferiors, they are too numerous to mention. Mr. Hangman Ellis told me of an English one who, only two or three decades ago, participated in the final ceremony and moved the fatal lever. He was particularly interested in certain physiological phenomena of which delicacy forbids mention here, but are well known to prison doctors and other eye-witnesses. James Joyce knew about them, as you may have read in *Ulysses*.

Executioners Risk their Lives

There is still another broad aspect of the office of public executioner which ought not to be overlooked in a treatise of this nature. In all countries there are times when the State executioner runs a certain personal risk. Towards the end of his career, our own Mr. Ellis had the humiliating task of hanging persons involved in Irish political troubles. Now the Irish are a pernicious, troublesome, resentful, and long-memoried race, and Mr. Ellis is not the only person whose life they have made a burden. He was often threatened and sometimes had to have police protection, and even to carry a revolver for his own safety. Note that Ireland pays England the delicate compliment of employing English hangmen; they cannot find one of their own in the Green Isle. The reason, I am told, is that in Ireland a hangman, even at the present moment, runs considerable risk and, like some film stars who shun publicity for publicity's sake, or important persons of royal blood, he has to travel *incognito*. Apropos Ireland, this is a country which in its long, turbulent history provided vast scope for England's hangmen, and one is hardly surprised to find that the Irish used to be "susceptible to hanging," as the Greeks are, to use their word for it, *prakskoppomatik*, which means "susceptible to political *coups d'état*." It is not uncommon to hear the proud boast of the ever-reminiscent patriotic Irishman that so many members of his family were hanged as rebels, for the old song says:

> They are hanging men and women
> For the wearing of the green!

—as if of an everyday occurrence, which, of course, it was quite often. Incidentally we read in Irish history of some interesting English refinements in the art for political ends. For example: "Men imprisoned on suspicion, or private information, were sometimes half-hanged or strangled almost to death before their guilt or innocence could be ascertained by trial."[20] *Half*-hanging! How very interesting!

Mr. Hangman Berry used to disguise himself as a woman every time he thought he ran a risk of being lynched by an inconsiderate mob, as, for example, when he was commissioned to break Mrs. Meybrick's neck. When we consider the nature of their calling, it is not surprising that public executioners both here and abroad are often threatened by denizens of the underworld, from which many of their clients are drawn. Of Deibler *père*, the most famous of French executioners, many stories are told of the risks he ran from dissatisfied "anarchists" and others upon whose friends he must needs operate. After the old man had removed the tiresome heads from Ravachol and several other anarchists, their companions swore that they would behead the surgeon himself. For a time the *Ministre de l'Intérieur* was at his wits' end to protect the unpopular public servant, and French logic was torn between the necessity for continuing to guillotine in broad daylight in an open space, as provided by law, and the necessity of saving Monsieur Deibler's life. To operate *La Veuve*, M. Deibler was indispensable. By law public execution was imperative. If M. Deibler ran the risk of being himself operated upon by the bombs of an excited and pernickety group of desperate anarchists: *Que faire?* Ceremony after ceremony was impaired. The unities and frankness of the whole business—ruined! Nevertheless, large numbers of pistolled and carbined *gendarmes* and *flics*, with cavalry often to help, gloriously upheld the grand tradition, and thus, by the grace of God, the public executions were performed during a very trying period of French history.

DRINKING THE PRISONER'S DOPE

When Deibler afterwards went to Corsica, it was expected that the hot-blooded Corsicans would never permit him to return alive to *La belle France*, but, to the astonishment of the authorities, his public appearances were a great success. Thousands flocked to Porto Vecchio to see the good "Widow" at work. So agitated was the executioner that once, inside the prison cell, after he had trimmed the condemned man's hair and shirt-neck (to remove a possible impediment to the operation of his blade) in a moment of agitation he drank the beaker of rum and dope that was mercifully to stupefy the criminal; and was hard put to it to fulfil his office with that dispatch and skill for which his name had become a by-word amongst our gallant Allies. Curiously enough, the French tend to regard hanging as barbarous. But then, is not everything that is not French barbarous to the French, even the language of Shakespeare?

It is hardly necessary for me to dwell upon this truth that public executioners and hangmen have had to run great risks in carrying out their duties, when we have these men as modern examples. Were I to quote all the incidents that I know of in which the executioner stood in grave risk of his life, I could fill many pages; perhaps one day I shall do so in a monumental work of biography to be entitled *The Lives of Great Executioners and Hangmen*.

IMPORTED HANGMEN

But it would hardly be fair to the reader for me to omit some mention of the really disgraceful way in which executioners were treated in modern Greece shortly after the introduction of capital punishment in that country. The Government sought for an executioner within its own frontiers, but found none. Two or three were imported from abroad, from a more humanitarian and civilized country. They were duly assassinated by an enraged populace. This, in itself, proves that modern Greece must have become a barbarous country, notwithstanding all the classicists may yammer about Greek culture, civilization and what not. Pshaw and fiddlesticks to them!—they cannot claim civilization or culture, or even common decency, for people who behave in such a manner towards a useful Civil Servant. An attempt was made to use soldiers as executioners—a little weakness of governments in such circumstances—but this the Senate would not permit. At last a man was found who would lend a willing hand to the work of human justice. He lived alone, far from Athens, in a fortress where he was guarded by soldiers. On the eve of an execution he was brought clandestinely in a vessel, and was hastily returned home as soon as his work was completed. Before, during, and after the exercise of his State functions he was surrounded by military to protect his life.

SPORTING INSTINCT OF THE GREEKS

At the time when the State was fortunate in finding the right man for the work, there were in prison between thirty and forty persons under sentence of death. These arrears were soon worked off. It appears that in Greece a condemned man was then permitted to defend his life; which goes to show that the modern Greeks have more sporting instinct than tendentious propaganda leads us to believe. The law ordained that he should walk freely to punishment, and that his hands should not be bound. Now, the greater part of those sentenced, brigands by profession, were vigorous men, who never failed to put up a valiant struggle with the executioner. Thus every execution began by a duel in which Justice always had the upper hand, being armed with a dagger. When the culprit had received eight or ten wounds, and had lost blood and strength, he usually went freely to execution. The account ends with the significant words:

> The people returned to the city asking themselves how
> they could best assassinate the executioner.[21]

I was surprised to find that so humane a man as Charles Dickens did not altogether approve of hanging and hangmen. He remarks that while all kinds of attention and consideration are lavished on the criminal, the hangman is universally avoided like a pestilence. And in this regard he asks:

> Is it because the hangman executes a law which when
> they once come near it face to face, all men instinctively
> revolt from?

Dickens was another of those unrealistic humanitarians (doubtful in his private life, so we hear) who, like John Bright, believed that security for human life is best to be found in a reverence for it. Did you ever hear anything so foolish or lacking in political sense?

Of course, Charles Dickens was a confirmed sentimentalist, and these words of his cannot by the most generous inter-pretation be considered as anything but disparaging to an official who, if not popular, ought to be. It is true that before the days of hanging in semi-secrecy, the hangman frequently wore a mask—to hide the benevolence of his countenance. It would hardly be good for the public to see him as a plain man like themselves; so he was made into a sort of bogey by the addition of a mask. The hangman can look us all in the face without a blush; and we ought to be able to look him straight in the face without a blush.

Hangman who Hanged his Brother

Why do we not accept the neck-breaking, throat-compressing strangler as a highly honoured and respected servant of our magnificent Governments? What perverted impulse drives the British public to pity the condemned man and to loathe the executioner? The great Spanish author Quevedo quotes a very common-sense letter from an uncle of his hero Paul.[22] This uncle was a man of virtuous leanings and well known in Segovia as a friend of the law; its final acts were "carried out" by him. He was in fact, the King's hangman. He wrote thus to his nephew:

> My dear Paul,
>
>   The weighty affairs of this employment (in which it has pleased his Majesty to place me) have prevented me from writing to you before this; for if there be any fault to find with the King's service, it is in the hard work it entails, which is, however, in some measure requited by the honour of serving him. It grieves me to have to send you unpleasant news: your father died a week ago, with as much bravery and resolution as ever man did. I speak from personal knowledge, having hoisted him myself ... On arrival at the gallows he set his foot on the ladder and climbed it nimbly, not crawling on all fours as some do; and, noticing that one of the rungs was cracked, he turned to the officers and ordered them to get it repaired for the next, because all men had not his spirit. I cannot express how well he impressed the onlookers. At the top of the ladder he sat down, shook the creases from his clothes,

took hold of the rope, made the noose, and then perceiving that the priest wished to preach, he turned to him and said, "Assume that your speech is ended: let us have a few staves of the Creed and have done quickly, for I hate to waste time." When this was done he charged me to put his cap a little to one side and to wipe his slaver, which I did; and then he swung without even doubling his legs or making a grimace, but kept such solemnity of countenance that nothing better could be desired. I quartered him and the highway was his sepulchre ... With your knowledge of Latin and rhetoric you will make an exceptional exponent of the hangman's art.

On His Majesty's Service

I quote this to show the difference between Dickens the sentimentalist and Quevedo the realist—note the reference to Latin and rhetoric. Quevedo, one of the great figures in world literature, had a just estimate of the hangman's importance in the social economy. The above is an account of a man who hanged his own brother, as a matter of duty, in the service of his God, his King, and his Country. There is not one atom of sentiment in it. That is how things ought to be. Note also the calm way in which the man took his hanging. And we speak of the romantic, excitable South! Tosh! In this country are we not ten times more sentimental? Think of the fuss we made of the Crumbles "romance," and of that of Mrs. Thompson and Bywaters; and of Monsieur Vaquier, who not long ago was dispatched to the bourne from which no man returns. And many others.

The Press and Crime

I now come to yet another aspect of hanging which is of great public interest. Earlier in this Handbook I have shown that not enough attention is paid to the hanging process. I have often thought that the newspaper Press in this country does not make the best of State trials in which the accused looks like a man that is to be hanged, or is suitable for hanging. It must be admitted that the newspapers do give some space to such cases; but not nearly enough. The drama of the law and the psychology of crime, and the sporting element that is inherent in all murder trials, are good reasons for allocating far more space than at present to details. Why should not an intelligent Press follow the life of a man accused of murder from his arrest either to the grave or acquittal, as the case may be? People who read the daily Press are men, women, and children of discrimination, and a public so highly educated and thoughtful as ours is surely not too sophisticated to be titillated by bon-bons of gossip from the condemned cell or succulent morsels of news from the gallows. The fare is good, moral, and elevating. The scheduled death always provides the right kind of sensation for the millionaire Press which is read by millions. No need to take very seriously what the psychologist Jung says, which is, believe it or not, that *capital punishment encourages rather than deters murderers*! Every man to be hanged is most excellent "copy"; every hanging is still better copy. In a democracy already sodden and saturated with sensation, in which a ridiculous sport such as dog-racing has to be invented from time to time, or some beastly kind of contortionism, either in the form of music or dance, has to be paraded on the stage, and in which a street accident will bring a crowd of morbid sightseers, is it right to neglect hangings as we do? The daily Press is, to the average Englishman, what the Colosseum was to the old Roman or the bull-ring is to the Spaniard: the chief thrills of life are to be found in it. The mental sadism from which the public suffers could be more adequately catered for than at present, and the freedom which our Press enjoys, and the good taste for which it is noted, should be exploited to the full. As one who has the interests both of English journalism and of hanging at heart, I propose to offer certain suggestions to the editors of our great newspapers, in order that they may better provide for the requirements of a news-loving public. The paper shortage in Britain due to World War II does not continue as we prepare for World War III.

HINTS FOR EDITORS

First, it is in the interests of Justice that newspapers should "follow up" every crime, and especially every capital crime. They should employ men of special talents and qualifications for this task, preferably men who are in close touch with the police; literate ex-criminals or ex-policemen might sometimes be trusted with this work. They should be paid liberally and given generous allowances for essential out-of-pocket expenses; any investigator will tell you that this is essential in all criminal inquiries. While these men are busy on the outside work following up the capital crime, the editorial staff should lose no time about getting ready the biography of the accused, and collect and collate full information in regard to his family, occupation, habits, and customs; the name of his club, of his favourite author and favourite tobacco; of his tailor if he is a "natty" man; and any other facts likely to be of the least interest. All this should be done in the greatest detail, and there need be no editorial false delicacy in withholding from print those little failings common to everybody, which everybody would hate to read of himself, but loves to read of others. The best must be made of the murder trial itself. Special artists, photographers, and writers with an eye for romance and a nose for sensation can always be commissioned. The human interest and the story are both of far more importance than accuracy in detail, and where the two collide, accuracy must go to the wall; the spirit, as in translation, is of greater importance than the letter. How deplorably some newspapers fail in regard to murder trials may be judged from the following table:

ENGLAND[23]

Publicity given to:	(A) *Murder Trial* (Kennedy & Brown)	(B) *Death of a great author* (Thomas Hardy)
DAILY NEWSPAPERS:	inches	inches
The Times	352	262
Daily Telegraph	361	320
Morning Post	304	432
Daily News	279	528
Daily Mail	336	180
Evening News	624	96
Star	386	86
Evening Standard	263	150
Daily Express	522	90
SABBATH NEWSPAPERS:		
Observer	22	182
Sunday Times	20	40
Sunday Dispatch	152	30
Sunday Express	42	48
Lloyds Sunday News	235	6
Reynolds News	240	12
News of the World	312	30

U.S.A.[24]

Publicity given to:	(A) *Murder Trial* (Snyder Case) inches	(B) *Death of a great author* (Thomas Hardy) inches
Herald-Tribune	54.5	59.0
New York Times	63.5	31.5

World	78.5	20.0
American	116.0	5.0
News (tabloid)	289.0	2.0

MAKING CRIME PAY

There is no better reading for Sunday than of crime and criminals, murders, and hangings; and nothing more appropriate. When the English working man has been to church or, alternatively, filled himself to the neck with beer and eaten the good roast beef of old Argentine, what more is necessary to keep holy the Sabbath than to read an account of some interesting romance, in which, for preference, a murder has been committed? The more religiously minded editors of our Sunday Press have, in some measure, a hazy idea of this profound truth, and there are many praiseworthy efforts of English journalism exuded from Fleet Street every Saturday night. We are frequently regaled with elaborate accounts of the life and astonishing adventures of men hanged, and they often provide much of real interest to the student of life and letters. Some good poetry in the newspaper sense would have been lost to the world had not an enterprising Sunday newspaper provided us with the *Memoirs* of the quite silly Monsieur Vaquier.

Editors may find on occasion that the condemned man is too depressed to write his autobiography, in which case the best course is to commission his wife or some other close relation or even a casual acquaintance to provide material for a ghosted story of it all.

MEMOIRS OF THE HANGED

The man who seems certain to hang—having been condemned to die—should have his whole past raked up; nothing should be left unstated, since he cannot defend himself against calumny. The public should note (and free-lance journalists should note) that the market for such memoirs is both vast and remunerative. In some cases as much as one hundred guineas or more have been paid per thousand words for the life story of a man awaiting execution. That of a woman is even more lucrative. Think of this, in comparison with the rewards for epic poetry, which is far more difficult to write. So long as there is one fact of interest in every twenty or thirty lines, the rest may be blown out; in most newspaper offices they keep gasbags for the purpose. An expert editorial staff will provide all the throbs and thrills and sensational details that are necessary. Inflation—journalistic inflation—need not be feared; as, indeed, it seldom is. We often have reason to believe that the hot-air pump is an essential part of the equipment of modern newspaper offices; and that experts in its use are not lacking. In the story of the condemned man's life we are mercifully freed from the tyranny of the happy ending. After his death there is no risk of libel. Dramatists, film- and detective-story writers, and others are envious that, in nine cases out of ten, the hangman dispatches the unwanted characters far more neatly than they do.

There is at present no serious periodical devoted exclusively to the interests of executioners—as there is to the interests of undertakers, funeral upholders, and directors—although obviously such a publication is badly needed. Many of our admirable publishing houses would, I am sure, consider the proposal if it were put to them in the form of a concrete project. Having deeply pondered the subject I am in a position to offer certain suggestions. First, as to title. The periodical should be called *The Hangman's Magazine and Executioner's Chronicle*. It should be conducted on the sound progressive lines of, say, *The Hairdresser*, or *Dogs*, *The New Statesman*, or *The Tailor and Cutter*. There should be short editorial notes of interest to hanging judges, sheriffs, prison employees, and executioners of all kinds, but especially hangmen.

The "Hangman's Record" Quoted

It is really appalling to think that, in this age of advanced science, we are so far losing touch with reality as to lose sight also of the need for some such publication as this. The latest attempt of which I can find any trace is the last issue of *The Hangman's Record*. My copy is dated 1926, and bears the blurbish subtitle: "All the principal Executions for 400 years. This Record, which has been specially compiled for the Publisher, contains Fuller Details and More Sensational Items than has ever before been issued to the Public. A Marvellous Book to settle a debate." It is not really a "book" but a large sixteen-page pamphlet in small print. It contains many laconic statements such as:

> 1554—Archbishop Cranmer was sentenced to death for High Treason. He was pardoned and sent to Oxford, where he was burnt in 1556.
> 1554—Sir Nicolas Throckmorton was tried for High Treason and found not guilty. The verdict was considered unsatisfactory and the jury were sent to prison and only released on paying very heavy fines.

Hangman's Magazine

Some 400 interesting hangings are listed in *The Hangman's Record*, which deserves to be brought up to date with all those post-Second World War hangings of war criminals of which we have read; and space can be reserved for the next lot. In the publication we have in mind, which should go much further than this simple Record, there always should be a good leading article on some matter of immediate importance to State killers, such as the (1948) strike of executioners in France. The periodical should, generally, try to advance the great cause of hanging; and agitate for better status, pay, and conditions for our public executioners. There should be a column of social gossip about leading hangmen, much information regarding their personal habits and idiosyncrasies could be included to the great advantage of posterity. (I find it ridiculously difficult to discover more than a few of the bare facts in the lives of great hangmen of the past.) There should be a special section devoted to new inventions and contraptions for use in dispatching criminals. There should be a Medical Column, in which new ideas tending to prove the instantaneousness of death, and the painlessness of hanging, could be well ventilated. There should be statistics of State killings throughout the world, with graphs showing rise or fall. There should be a technical section on the dynamics, ballistics, hydrostatics, and electronics of execution. Whether it would or would not be wise to include an occasional note on bungled executions must, of course, depend upon public policy: perhaps they could better be filed as top secrets for official use only, as in the past. There should above all be a section for the review of books such as this, so that the world could have the benefit of expert criticism. At present criticism must necessarily be of the lay kind, and therefore almost valueless. One does not look to *The Times Literary Supplement* for criticism of a book on pinking, bobbing, or shingling: and therefore one ought not to have to rely upon it for reviews of books on capital punishment or hanging. There should be in every number a short story on a theme in some ways bearing upon hanging or execution. Strictly speaking, the hangman ought always to be the hero of such stories.

There ought also to be a section for serial fiction, and for this there are many books already in existence which would be eminently suitable. I have no doubt at all that had the late Mr. Edgar Wallace or Mr. Kipling been approached (in the right manner) they could have found both the time and the inspiration to provide the best type of serial. We still have with us Mr. J.B. Priestley and Mr. Graham Greene—and there are many lesser literary panjandrums who would come forward if terms were good. In the U.S.A. there are many fine writers who could do just as well—or better, because they are less inhibited than the British. Hanging could usefully be more often introduced into that paying formula of the modern novelist: sex, sadism, and sentimentalized religion. It is well worth considering. And the Order of Merit should be given for the best literary execution, as it has been on at least one occasion in the past.

That suitable material must be lying about in bottom drawers somewhere is certain—as I shall now show.

THE PIERREPONT PAPERS QUOTED

Like the Sansons in France, the Pierrepoints of England have been hereditary hangmen, and one of them, the late Thomas William Pierrepoint, uncle of the recently retired Albert the Famous, used often to go to Ireland in answer to requests for his services. The Sheriff of Dublin County was a Mr. MacCracken, and this gentleman approached T. W. Pierrepoint in November 1923, a time of great troubles in the Green Isle, asking him to come over and do a job. There was an exchange of business correspondence[25] in which the English executioner (very much *persona non grata* over there) showed himself to be a good chap and utterly without either that malice for which Dublin conversation is notable, or the not always occult malice for which politics, Irish and English, is often deplorable. Pierrepoint provides interesting information about his *modus operandi* as regards his kit and dangerous travelling. In one letter, after saying: "... I shall always be very pleased to Oblige and to do my best for any Gentleman who inquires for me with pleasure, Sir," he adds this P.S.: "I arrived home quite safe and without any trouble I had a good look around Dublin while [sic] into the afternoon and then walked part way to Kingstown and got into a tram the remainder of the way and booked across from Kingstown I kept hearing conversations about the execution at Mountjoy but I never let on even the sailors on boad [sic] were looking out for the hangman and I was close behind them but I never let on I expect they thought of seeing me with a lot of luggage but I never carry any with me only in my pocket a pair of pliers a two foot rule and tape measure as I think it better than carrying a hand bag I think it gives the game away I believe in going nice and quiet about my business and not let everybody know who I am." Apparently another Irish Sheriff—and at Christmas too!—treated him rather shabbily: on this he wrote more in sorrow than in anger, explaining in a "post-script" the better treatment he received in England: "Over here if we get notified of a reprieve before we leave home we do not expect to get anything unless they wish to send a small sum for Expenses of writing I have had a retainer of £300 and I have had as low as 10/– for expenses of writing but if we get to the Prison before we get to know of a reprieve we get paid in full as if we had carried out the Execution ..." *Aha*! The usually generous Irish had been more cheeseparing than the usually tight-fisted English officialdom! Pierrepoint's way of putting things was tactful, even delicate. It is reported that an Irish prison governor kept a condemned man waiting at the gallows while he argued with another imported hangman from England about an extra fiver demanded (possibly "danger money" in that Irish atmosphere). We do not have enough in the way of hangmen's correspondence to make up what would be a very revealing anthology. English executioners have a reputation for discretion of which they have every reason to be proud.

This Thomas Pierrepoint used to help out Scottish authorities in moments of difficulty, for, like Ireland, Scotland has no corps of hangmen of its own: a grave weakness in an otherwise strong country. Some correspondence between him and Sir John Samuel was published in 1956. In September 1925, Pierrepoint wrote about one John Keen, who had been sentenced to death. "I have," he said, "great pleasure in offering my services to you for the execution of the above named man," and then he sketched his outstanding qualifications for the job, adding: "Hoping you will consider me, as I have been engaged before at Glasgow, but have never had the pleasure of coming as they have all been reprieved." *Always at your service*—this seems to have been the Pierrepoint motto. It is recorded of Thomas Pierrepoint that, rather than miss participation in Christmas festivities at home, he turned down an offer of a hanging made by the Glasgow authorities who quite forgot the English respect for Christmas, this being overshadowed in their minds by thoughts of Hogmanay, that is New Year's eve, which is to them much more important. All Scots would prefer haggis to hanging.

Nobody can say that this amiable man did not enjoy his little trips. He did good work too.

THE CONDEMNED MAN

It is a difficult problem for prison authorities to find ways and means of amusing men who are awaiting strangulation, and I doubt my own ability to do so. As a rule condemned men are hard to please. An approved system is to overwhelm them with religious advice and consolation, which takes the form of prayers and exhortations to repentance and faith in the glorious life to come. This, far from being an entertainment, is much too depressing and if there is one man on this earth who deserves to be amused it is the unfortunate wretch under sentence of death. Heaven, we understand, is dull; and hell is uncomfortable. There are, however, many pleasant indoor games and recreations which are in every way suitable as a means of passing the weary hours, days, and weeks that intervene between the final decision of the Court of Criminal Appeal and the morning on which the State gives a man his quietus. One suitable game, well within the intelligence of most prisoners, is *Snakes and Ladders*, and there are scores of others. Furthermore, there is much good literature relevant to the conditions of men that are to take the drop (or be "turned off" as the Newgate Calendar elegantly expresses it). Victor Hugo wrote an effective and entertaining book, *The Last Days of a Condemned Man*. In 1950 there appeared in Britain an illuminating work by George Riley Scott full of choice anecdotes about the old hangmen on the national scroll of honour. In the rich and honest past it was easy to collect information about hanging and hangmen. Not so today, when the State makes every possible effort to keep the whole business dark; and the contemporary hangman is the very soul of discretion from the State point of view. No servants of the State, not even those Nardacs of science entrusted with Research for Destruction by Atomization and Vaporization, have to be more careful of their life, habits, and conversation.

Note on the Literature of Hanging

Dickens and Thackeray wrote a fair amount about crime, criminals, and hangings; the American, Ambrose Bierce, wrote masterly short stories of a type that would tend to bring comfort to a man nearing death. And then there is *The Infamous John Friend*, by Mrs. R.S. Garnett, a book which (I am glad to see) is recognized for what it is worth; it concludes with a magnificent imaginative description of the feelings of a man that was hanged. It is also encouraging to see that some of the more intelligent of our modern writers have not overlooked the literary possibilities in the hangman's art. Mr. William Gerhardi has given us a wonderful long-short story, *A Bad End*, in which he displays a subtle and delicate appreciation of the final ceremony; the execution in this tale is an admirable conception. But it is to a young lady of marked talents and great promise that the palm must be awarded for the first full-length novel with a hangman as hero. *Hanging Johnny*, by Miss Myrtle Johnson, if written in French, would certainly have been crowned by the Academy. *A Hangman's Diary*, by Franz Schmidt, translated by C. Calvert and A.W. Gainer, is well worth perusal by all who are interested in the art. All such works are to be highly commended as tending to a dissemination of knowledge about hanging; and it is to be hoped that we shall have more in the same vein. However, fiction is not enough. What is really necessary is something more serious. A German writer, Dr. Else Angstmann, has made a good beginning with her treatise, *Der Henker in der Volksmeinung* ("Public Opinion and the Hangman"); in this book a magnificent bibliography of the subject is given. What we urgently need is an English Spengler to write a philosophic History of State killings—Arnold Toynbee could make it an Appendix to his useful *Study of History*—and I have no doubt but that such a work would have to be called *The Decline of Hanging*. The truth is we are in the diminuendo stage of an art which once swung forward in a grand crescendo. Sappho wrote:

Where hath my maidenhead flown?

My friend Dylan Thomas would have been justified in giving us some of his resounding verse under the title:

Incredibiliter delector

—and there are, of course, the Sitwells—very reliable literary people. Best of all would be T.S. Eliot, O.M., who has shown himself to be deeply interested in murder, especially that murder in the cathedral of which so much has been written. He has the right mind for the poetry of hanging.

HANGING ON STAGE AND SCREEN

It is, at least, satisfactory to observe that there was between the two World Wars a revival of the fine old melodrama in which fornication and death are the stock ingredients. *Maria Marten, or The Murder at the Red Barn*, was played to crowded houses; *Sweeney Todd, or The Demon Barber of Fleet Street*, also did well. *The Beggar's Opera* is rather *too* frivolous, but the old music is delightful. And now we have a musical (*Belle*) on the life of Dr. Crippen, a victim of hanging for love. Cinematograph producers have neglected the possibilities, not of murder and violence, but of executions. The film *Dawn*, of high entertainment value, was a bright spot on the horizon until 1950, when it was eclipsed by *Kind Hearts and Coronets*, already mentioned. But best of all was the French film *Nous sommes Tous des Assassins* (1952). This film must make us all pause to think, for it does something which we have not yet done in England: shows everything that happens on the morning of execution, except the actual execution. Today *La Veuve* ("The Widow," as the humorous French call their guillotine) is a streamlined machine-tooled engine that is carried around France for the decapitations in a polished black three-ton lorry. It removes an average of forty heads a year, and the Master of Ceremonies who operates the guillotine bears the traditional name of Monsieur de Paris (reminding us of the Comte de Paris, on the higher social scale). The Widow drops at dawn. At 3:50 four warders take off their shoes and tip-toe to the condemned cell. The door is flung open and the man who is to die is pinned down with no chance to fight or shout. Then comes the prison governor to speak the dry formula, "You must be very, very brave." And then begins the last walk down a dim-lit corridor, past the priest with his portable altar, offering the Last Sacrament. Next is the prison barber, a cynical character with a cigarette-butt stuck to his lower lip, giving a swift shave to the condemned man's neck. Finally, hands and feet tied, the condemned man is dragged the last few yards to the guillotine. The film shows it all—up to the curtained door beyond which the Widow waits.

This moving film was written and produced by Maître André Cayette, a distinguished lawyer who has been present at five executions. It is a very powerful film, so powerful that in France its exhibition was prohibited or limited to select audiences. The moral is simple. We simply must make a film of a hanging, if only to reassure the public that we order things better here than they do in France. André Cayette made no money out of his film, but otherwise it was a great success. The financial results of most of these enterprises have been good, I understand; so that although the art of State killing may itself show a steady decline, there is no real reason why it should be ignored by the stage, the cinematograph, or the printing press. Were it not that the present compiler is rushing publication of this book (so that he may proceed to an exegesis on that interesting apocryphal character Nahum the Elkoshite), many other instances could be quoted to show that the British public thoroughly enjoys murders and executions; and especially hangings—if they are well and neatly done.

STILL MORE MISTAKES OF HANGMEN

Earlier in this book several instances were quoted of bunglings and failures by hangmen in their work. It is opportune that a few more be now introduced, to refresh the mind of the reader and to prevent him from losing his sense of proportion. There was the case of a gentleman named Patrick Harnet, of whom it is written:

> As the body dropped to a standstill a heavy gurgling sound was heard, and soon the blood in torrents commenced pouring on the stone floor below. The cap was raised and it was found that decapitation was almost complete, the head hanging to the body only by a small piece of skin at the back of the neck. During the half-minute or more that the heart beat, the blood was thrown against the platform above from the exposed gash caused by the head being pulled back on the shoulder.

Can we not visualize the scene? Doubtless, at the first smile of dawn on the morning of this execution, when the early rays of Apollo were beginning to gild the hill-tops, the official hangman kicked his wife out of bed and said to her: "Fry me a couple of eggs, dearie, and a rasher or so of bacon. I have important work to do for the Government this morning, and I must therefore eat a good breakfast." There must necessarily have been weakness in the hangman's technique in this case. But, nevertheless, the effect upon the prisoner was the same as if the beau idéal—i.e. dislocation of the neck—had been achieved. There is also the case of the late Mr. John Coffey, of whom it is reported:

> When the drop fell the rope broke and the body fell to the ground. The neck was not broken, but the shock caused the blood to spurt from the wretched man's ears. He was carried back ... and while the rope was being adjusted, he regained consciousness and begged to have the cap removed and make another speech. The rope broke a second time, but the body was caught before it reached the ground. It was lifted up and held in place by Deputy Sheriffs while the noose was again adjusted. The rope held and Coffey was strangled to death, dying in twelve minutes.

Time is not the essence of the contract in hanging; as already pointed out, the judicial sentence is "To be hanged by the neck *until* dead." For this reason it is now customary, in order to compensate for possible miscalculations, to leave the hanged man's body suspended for the best part of an hour; thus, if his neck is not broken, he is certain to die from strangulation. The net result in every case is the same, from the point of view of prisoner and public: the man, woman, or infant is killed, which is all that matters. The State is satisfied, even when nobody else is.

ALL SORTS MAKE MISTAKES—EVEN EXPERTS

I feel that, in the accounts I have given of mistakes by hangmen, I may have conveyed to the reader an impression that they are the *only* people concerned with the elimination of undesirables who make mistakes. Nothing could be further from my mind. In the literature of the Law and State killings there is sufficient information to fill several anthologies, showing that almost everybody concerned with the killing has at some time or another plunged into the grossest error. It is therefore a happy thought that, once an accused person has been dispatched by the hangman, difficult questions about his guilt seldom arise. The law is satisfied, the hangman has probably spent his fee; and that is usually enough. The worst mistakes are those made by "expert witnesses," who are usually medical doctors specializing in morbid pathology. Few of these expert witnesses, in trials when a man's life may depend on their testimony, will admit the truth: that their science is still in the seminal stage. Many of them are ready to dogmatize like priests as if they were defending a question of pure faith when it is more often than not one of facts found and/or mere *opinion*. Nothing is more entertaining to the non-expert than to listen to one of these learned men combat another in the witness-box:

> For ev'n though vanquished he could argue still;
> While words of learned length and thundering sound ...

What is even more entertaining is for you or me to read what expert witnesses of, say, fifty years ago said, and then compare it with knowledge representing the present state of their science. How utterly bogus much of it seems today! It causes us to wonder whimsically what people of fifty years hence will think of the learned evidence now being submitted by our contemporary experts! An appalling thought crosses our minds: Is it, as time generally proves it to be, mostly hallucination and nonsense? In the Year of Grace 1936, in England, a lady named Mrs. Bryant was hanged for the murder of her husband by arsenic poisoning. Evidence was submitted to show that a tin said to have contained arsenic had been burned by her in a copper fire. The ashes were analyzed and found to contain 149.6 parts of arsenic in a million, which, the learned expert said, *proved that arsenic had been put on the fire*. Another learned man, a Professor at The Imperial College of Science and Technology, and one of the greatest of our authorities on fuels and their residues, read of this matter of arsenic in the ashes. Arsenic in ashes? Why, the Professor knew that *all* coal-ash contains arsenic! He would see to it that that item of expert evidence did not pass unchallenged. But the Court of Appeal refused to hear him: no doubt on perfectly solid legal grounds. What must have been the effect of the expert evidence upon a jury of laymen at the original trial? The number of accused is legion, and many of them have been executed on expert evidence, much of it highly suspect. Is not this admirable from the hangman's point of view?

Hangmen Not Concerned with Errors of Courts

Some were reprieved—to be found innocent: Adolf Beck, for instance, who took *nine years* to establish his innocence. In his case the expert's evidence seemed to be overwhelming and irrefutable, and other evidence substantiated it. Lord Shaw of Dunfermline, one of our finest judges, quotes a case of a man called Dogherty as such a flagrant instance of wrongful conviction and execution that, from that moment, the learned judge ceased to believe in capital punishment: wrongly, no doubt, for one swallow does not make a summer, nor *one* bad picture an Exhibition of the Royal Academy. William Habron, as you know, was sentenced to death for a murder afterwards confessed to by the late Mr. Charles Peace. The late Mrs. Biggadyke was hanged for a murder for which a man confessed on his deathbed. And there was Tomka, who, in 1923, was hanged for murder, only to be proved innocent by expert witnesses—in 1927. Jacobowski was executed in 1926 and another man was proved in 1929 to have been guilty of the crime. Other cases could be cited,[27] but they make rather depressing reading, especially for our hangmen, who are not really concerned with matters of guilt and who, no doubt, prefer to think of a Court of Law as an infallible institution. But let one thing be quite clear: these doubts of guilt and proofs of innocence of executed persons must not be taken to reflect upon the integrity—the absolute and unchallengeable integrity—of our hangmen. If they occasionally make mistakes, strangle instead of asphyxiate or neck-break or vice versa, or pull off an occasional head, such incidents are mere accidents. Do we not all sometimes get out of the wrong side of the bed of a morning?

Hanging in the U.S.A

As hanging today is fundamentally an English art and speciality, little attention need be given in these pages to hanging in other countries. Yet offence might be taken where none is meant if I were to ignore entirely the hanging which continues in certain parts of Britain's lusty child, the United States of America. I do not refer to those crude and irresponsible affairs called lynchings, because they can only be regarded as amateurish, and, besides, what we are dealing with here is State killing with the full authority of the law and the approval of a civilized community behind it. Nothing is more painful for the present writer than to have to record that few of the American hangmen are anything like as proficient in the art as their English compeers. Yet, in justice, it cannot be said that the Americans *bungle* more hangings than the British. In fairness, and on behalf of Britain's American friends, it must be pointed out that, where hanging is used for State killing in the U.S.A., far too little attention is paid to the principle "dislocation of the neck is the ideal to be aimed at." If the present work should help to drive this point home, I have not the slightest doubt but that the Americans, not a slow people to learn, would soon show themselves to be as proficient as the British. Meanwhile their attitude towards hanging deserves some attention, and although I could fill many pages with well-authenticated examples to illustrate when, where, and how American hangmen have been behind the British, I have no desire to labour this aspect of the subject, lest a deep and important international friendship be impaired at a critical moment in the power-history of the world. In a book with the engaging title, *Loafing Round the Globe*, written by the German Richard Katz, and translated by Gerald Griffin, the author interviewed an American sheriff and, when it came to hanging, he asked this question: "Do you carry out the execution yourself, Sheriff?" The sheriff replied: "Of course we do it ourselves, myself and my men. We have no hangmen to help us. If the murderer is tractable and relaxes his muscles, he is killed instantaneously. Otherwise he does a bit of jazzing in the air. He takes somewhere about five minutes to finish his capering. However, *that is his own fault*. Don't blame *us*. *We* are not cruel. In fact, if he wants to make a little speech or sing a song before the white cap is adjusted, we give him time to do so. You should be here to see us giving them their send-off. The next batch will be tied up in October."

Most instructive, this. No professional hangman to officiate. Jazzing in the air. Five minutes to finish capering. "All his own fault." "Don't blame us." One would not dream of blaming the sheriff and his men, who, on the sheriff's showing, always do their best to make a good go of the job. But where blame, if any, rests is with the educational authorities who do not see that sheriffs and their men are taught the art of hanging as it is practiced by the smarter modern English executioners. Wherever I look among accounts of American hangings I find something to indicate a certain lack of dispatch. Yet there is one great comfort: America's hanged die as certainly as England's. In one respect the Americans far surpass the English: they do not make such a hole-and-corner business of hanging in the United States as they do in Britain, where today one well-trained and highly discreet Press representative is the only person outside officialdom permitted to be present.

THE SIX WHO WERE HANGED

Some years ago an American friend sent me a little book with the title *The Six Who Were Hanged*, by Clem G. Hearsey. The author gives his own eye-witness account of the historic hangings at Amite, La., on 9th May, 1924, when six men paid the extreme penalty on the gallows for the murder of one. The men were guilty in accordance with the law. But the hangings could have been better done, or so it seems. Three scenes of the actual executions which took place are reproduced from photographs taken on the spot at the time; they must be among the most unusual photographs in the world. I shall not dwell on those visual horrors, but content myself with a few brief extracts from the book relating to those memorable hangings:

> Late Thursday night Captain Rennyson arrived from New Orleans in an automobile. He brought the 100 feet of rope with which the men were to be hanged, and which had been stretched in the prison at New Orleans. His companion on the journey was Joe the Hangman. Joe, a bowed man, with stiff, sandy hair, short gray mustache, tobacco-stained, and fiercely bushy eyebrows, is a sort of "jack" carpenter and iron-worker of New Orleans. He is 61 years old, lives in Carrollton, and before hanging these Italians had hanged ten or a dozen men in the Parish Prison in New Orleans. As a hangman he is a butcherly worker, and has such little skill that his victims are lucky

indeed if their necks break on the drop. He is callous and hardened as is natural for a man of his trade, and when on a "job," as he terms it, must have a drink of whisky every now and then …

The sheriff did everything he possibly could for his prisoners and allowed them all they asked for in the way of food or such considerations as a prison may afford.

All through the morning there was an air of suppressed excitement, and Captain Rennyson, who had volunteered to assist Sheriff Bowden, and give expedition to the woe-weighted ceremony, was busy with the preparations. Early, Joe the Hangman came from his hiding-place in the prison kitchen, nimbly climbed the gallows and set the ropes above the two traps. The double-rope was coiled in two lengths of fifty feet and fitted to the staples over the traps. Joe, his face hidden by his black mask, deftly made his nooses and retired to the kitchen where he clamored loudly for a drink of whisky. All the whisky that could be obtained had been given to the condemned men as occasional stimulant during the night just passed, and the hangman had to content himself with strawberry wine. It was not to his palate.

At a few minutes before 12 o'clock Leona and Deamore were brought from their cells and their hands manacled behind their backs …

Three steps at a time the masked hangman ran up the gallows and first rushed to Deamore to groom him for the hard passing. Deamore stood impassive as the hangman wrapped the strands of rope about his legs, and attached cords to his manacled wrists. Leona on the other hand turned and watched the deathsman at his task … The two bodies fell, came up with a sudden jerk which visibly stretched the neck several inches … It was clean, quick work from the hangman's standpoint.

Giglio and Rini felt the summons before they heard it … The hangman crouched like an ugly poison spider between the two, raised his lever, and crash went the double traps ... Rini hung motionless, but Giglio spun twice on the rope, and vented a deep and long-sustained groan as his chest heaved and his shoulders and arms were drawn up in an ugly movement. Giglio groaned again, and there was a wheezing gurgle in his throat as he gasped for breath. His chest rose and fell rapidly, and his wrists twisted and turned as though trying to free themselves of the manacles, but soon the body seemed to stretch downwards and then it hung as motionless as Rini's. Although Giglio's showed evidence of strangulation ... the men were pronounced dead in less than fifteen minutes.

In the baggage car on the evening train going to New Orleans were six coffins and each contained the corpse of a hanged man. Deamore's neck was so swollen and distorted that the undertakers used more than a hundred pounds of ice to reduce the ugly folds of discoloured flesh. The rope had mangled Deamore's neck, and had the drop been greater, the man's head might have been torn from his shoulders.

So ended the awful hangings at Amite.

There is no need for comment, except to say that Joe the Hangman was not an artist but a very roughneck type of executioner. How he ever got the job one cannot understand, unless it was by political influence. Nobody can say that this sort of thing and the mess made of Deamore are good for hanging. But I believe I have said enough to show that, although America has something to learn from Old England in regard to this public function, the highly important fact remains: even a *bad* hanging does the work which the State demands. The person hanged *always* dies, however slowly. And so all is as well in the U.S.A. as in the British Commonwealth.

It seems rather absurd that some people should object to State killing being a long-drawn-out affair. Nobody has yet determined the *actual moment of death in any form of execution*. A distinguished scientist[28] writes of a decapitation:

> Immediately after the head was severed and dropped into the basket, I took charge of it. The facial expression was that of great agony, for several minutes after decapitation. He would open his eyes, also his mouth, in the process of gaping, as if he wanted to speak to me, and I am positive he could see me for several seconds after the head was severed from the body. There is no doubt that the brain was still active ... His decapitated body, which was previously fastened by a strap upon a bench, was in continuous spasmodic and clonic convulsions, lasting from five to six minutes, also an indication of great suffering.

Death Never Instantaneous

If this sort of thing happens when a body is beheaded, what happens when the neck is broken or strangulation takes place? Is it possible for any scientist *to prove* that death is instantaneous? The probabilities are in ninety-nine cases out of a hundred that in hanging it takes several minutes. Nor is there any proof of unconsciousness during the process: nobody who has died has ever yet been able to give us a description of what it is like. It is extremely doubtful if more than a tenth of one percent of the population would be really interested to know. So why worry?

All this was brought into closer focus by disclosures at a coroner's inquest in England in 1950, as reported in the *Daily Mail* of 5th April of that year. A man named Frank William Clemas collapsed just before an operation. His heart *stopped beating*. In English law a man is presumed dead after his breathing and circulation have stopped for five minutes. In this case a surgeon opened the abdomen and massaged the dead man's heart. *After eighteen minutes it began to beat again.*

Artificial respiration, drugs, and an injection were tried. After massaging, Frank William Clemas "gasped and began to breathe normally." But he died three days later. In other words Clemas died—legally—twice. An interesting speculation arises from this case. How many of the hanged could be brought back to consciousness again? We do not know, because official statistics are not available showing the number of those who died by strangulation and those who died from dislocation of the neck. Such statistics would not be in the interests of the hangmen. There is one comfort in it all, which is that almost anything can be proved or disproved by statistics. And there is always that great human safeguard: the person hanged is left hanging for long enough after he has been given the drop to make sure that he has died. So there is, after all, no great cause for worry. If, to this very day in our Welfare Britain, there are cases—how many, official secrecy, that is decency, prevents us from ever knowing— of slow death, they were quite common in the good old Merrie England of which we read. In 1740 William Duell was hanged and his body taken to Surgeons' Hall to be dissected. When he was laid on the board (says the *Gentleman's Magazine*, Vol. X, p.570) one of the servants "perceived life in him and found his breath come quicker and quicker." Margaret Dickson (known as "Half-hanged Meg") was hanged in 1728 but did not die until 1753, and Anne Green, hanged at Oxford in 1650, lived to see the year 1659. But, on the whole, hanging worked well, for we read in the same delightful publication (*Gentleman's Magazine*, Vol. LVIII, p.361, 1788) of some malefactors hanged at Newgate: "After hanging the usual time, they were taken down and the machine cleared away in half an hour. *By practice the art is much improved* AND THERE IS NO PART OF THE WORLD WHERE VILLAINS ARE HANGED IN SO NEAT A MANNER AND WITH SO LITTLE CEREMONY." That's more like our modern England, but, as we know, doing without ceremony was found to be unsatisfactory: a less light-hearted, more impressive, in fact more ceremonious method was found to be better.

SAVING "L'HONNEUR DE LA BELLE FRANCE"

Returning now to the subject of decapitation by the guillotine, I might as well mention one other not irrelevant case. A Frenchman was sitting in a prison cell awaiting execution (*avoir la tête tranchée*, as they say) and when the morning came he was confessed, bound, his hair cut, and he was marched off to the guillotine. The priest delivered him over to the executioner, who placed his patient in position for operation. The lever was pulled, to let loose the axe, and to quote an excellent account of the matter:

> The heavy triangle of iron slowly detached itself, falling by jerks down the slides until, horrible to relate, it wounded the man without killing him. The poor creature uttered a frightful cry. The disconcerted executioner hauled up the axe and let it slide down again. A second time the neck of the malefactor was wounded without being severed. Again he shrieked, the crowd joining in. The executioner raised the axe a third time, but no better effect attended the third stroke ...

Hoc opus, hic labor est.

In fact, it was a case like that of our celebrated true-born Englishman John Lee, "The Man they Couldn't Hang," to give him his film title. But with this difference, that the French executioner's assistant, after a few of these distressing and humiliating efforts of his chief, saved the honour of France by springing upon the unguillotined malefactor and "slowly cut through the neck with a knife." What a messy business! In a hanging, if a man does not take the drop effectively, the hangman can simply go into the drop-pit, seize his client's legs, and give them a few sharp tugs. This usually does the trick; and it is altogether a *clean* business, as befits the English sense for the aesthetic. Besides, there is the other great safeguard; one can always help the poor struggler to die by leaving him to hang for a period. This is now, and long has been, the standard English safeguard. It is infallible.

What would Dr. Guillotin, the *médecin aristocrat* and humanitarian, have thought of the crude butchery quoted, plagiarist that he was of the good old English Halifax Gibbet—that wonderful decapitating machine which Guillotin submitted as his own invention to solve the execution problem of the French Revolution?

DISGRACEFUL PLAGIARISM EXPOSED

Here I would pause for a moment and introduce a note which is not wholly creditable to executioners as a class. The natural pride which they have in their trade, art, or office has often an unseemly background of dishonesty, in that they often claim to have invented gadgets to expedite their work, whereas instead of being original inventors they have merely looked up and plagiarized some forgotten but useful or inspiring idea. The guillotine, that fascinating instrument favoured by the most logical of cultured peoples, and claimed by and for Dr. Guillotin, is a good illustration of this. Actually the beheading machine was a very old idea, no doubt based upon the Gules,[29] mentioned so far back as 1678 in Randle Holme's *Academy of Armoury*. A family (name not mentioned) bore it heraldically, and it is described thus: "GULES: a heading block fixed between two supporters, and an axe placed therein; on the sinister side a maule, *all proper*." Holme adds: "... this way of decollation was by laying the neck of the malefactor on the block, and then setting the axe upon it, which lay in a rigget (i.e. groove) on the two side-posts or supporters. The executioner, with the violence of a blow on the head of the axe with his heavy maule (mallet), forced it through the man's neck into the block."

From the "Gules" to the *machine à décapiter* by way of the Halifax Gibbet is not difficult engineering. The point is that Dr. Guillotin claimed the idea as his own! There is even one more discreditable feature of this plagiarism to be recorded. It was really a man named Laquiante of Strasbourg who stole the idea, and Guillotin cribbed it *from him*! The full credit for making a model of the "new" machine, however, must be given to a modest but intelligent and imaginative maker of pianofortes named Schmidt;[30] it was Schmidt's model or archetype which provided the full scientific basis for the machine finally used in the revolutionary decapitations—which machine, with a few manufacturing but no mechanical improvements, is used in France to this very day. I am glad to have been able, by virtue of careful historical research, to straighten this matter out. Let honour be given where honour is due, and it is unfair that the French should have plagiarized, stolen, adapted, and used an idea for eliminating undesirables humanely which is at core essentially English. It is true that the English may have plagiarized the idea from the Italian *mannaia*; and the Italians may have taken it from some other equally enlightened nation. There is nothing new under the sun, and in matters of capital punishment man has shown that he is always ready to learn from either friend or foe; and that, like many authors, he does not always acknowledge the sources of his inspiration.

The public decapitations during the French Revolution provided for the people a circus that was enjoyed almost as much as the old Roman circus. To what heights of ingenuity man can rise on encouraging occasions! But is it not extraordinary how often the key men in such entertainments are made to suffer by so unworthy a factor as bad pay and conditions? Citizen Sanson, France's No. 1 executioner, immortalized for his great work, gave voice to many a *cri de cœur*, one being the ideological lamentation that "... the abolition of class prejudices, I thought, would make it easier for me to find assistants, but on the contrary ..." and so on. One's heart breaks to think of the dilemmas which had to be faced by so unambivalent a man as Sanson. Thank God we have no such class prejudices in England!

ELECTROCUTION IS TORTURE

Hanging, as the English know, is certainly a much better method of execution than beheading—it is far less painful for onlookers.

I should be wanting in method if I did not say something about the electric chair, for which great claims are advanced in certain of the United States of North America. A French scientist is of the opinion, based upon a profound knowledge of electricity and its physiological effects, that the electric chair is the most inhuman form of execution conceived by the mind of man.

He says:

> In every case of electrocution, in the way in which Ruth Schneider and Judd Gray were executed (they are reported to have been subjected to 2,200 volts), death inevitably supervenes but it may be very long, and above all, excruciatingly painful ... the space of time before death supervenes varies according to the subject. Some have a greater physiological resistance than others. I do not believe that anyone killed by electrocution dies instantly, no matter how weak the subject may be. In certain cases death will not have come about even though the point of contact of the electrode with the body shows distinct burns. Thus, in particular cases, the condemned person may be alive and even conscious for several minutes without it being possible for a doctor to say whether the victim is dead or not ... This method of execution is a form of torture.[31]

An eminent pathologist, a man of great reputation and unequalled knowledge of his subject, has verbally confirmed this opinion to the compiler of the present book. He states that very often the real executioner in those States where electrocution is fashionable is the doctor who does the post-mortem examination. Electrocution is unsportsmanlike, and the smell of frying human flesh in the immediate neighbourhood of the chair is sometimes bad enough to nauseate even the Press representatives who are present.

Amos O. Squire, M.D., Chief Physician of Sing Sing, who, before he wrote what follows, had attended the electrocution of 138 persons, says that when the signal is given, "a sound comes from the electrician's niche—not unlike the sound of an X-ray apparatus, a cackle, whine, and buzz. The figure in the chair gives one terrific lurch against the straps, every muscle contracting and straining. The face—all that can be seen from mouth to throat—turns crimson. Sometimes a wisp of smoke rises from the top of the head, and with it the smell of burning ... After a few seconds the current is cut off ... the doctor with his stethoscope listens for heartbeats—he listens to them *grow fainter and fainter*. A brief interval passes. The switch is thrown again—and after contact is broken, again the doctor listens. There is *seldom* any pulse this time ..." The words in italics are mine—"fainter and fainter" and then another dose of current, after which there is "seldom"—*seldom*, mark you—any pulse. That is if all goes well. But does not an electricity supply, even a good one such as that of the London Underground Railway system, sometimes behave in a disconcerting manner? To quote Dr. Squire again: "The terrific current causes instantaneous contraction of all muscles in the body, resulting in severe contortions of the limbs, fingers, toes, face, and protrusion of the eyes. If applied for as long as half a minute, burning rapidly develops at the point of contact, and a post-mortem examination shows eyes in a foggy condition 'with a star fracture of the lens, heart dilated and filled with fluid blood ... in about five percent of cases in a contracted or tetanized condition ... I have seen two cases where the heart was ruptured,'" etc., etc.—and the doctor concludes, "In comparing electrocution with hanging as a means of inflicting the death penalty, I believe that electrocution *is more humane and certain and less painful*."[32]

Well, well, well! As if it is possible for any Englishman to swallow that story—more humane and less painful than hanging! Impossible and vainglorious statement, incapable of the least proof! We cannot and must not admit it for one moment: the honour of Britain is at stake. It is all very well for quibblers to say that both forms of execution are, to say the least, a little unpleasant at times for the onlookers. But the hangman is, nevertheless, a superior being in every way to the "electrocutioner," for, as we have seen earlier, he is an artist depending upon intuition and personal skill and not upon a mere electric current for the success of his work.

In the hangman there is a much more human and personal service element: which is as it should be in these painful affairs.

A Needle Through the Head

That electrocution is not always painless for onlookers was proved once more in the recent and famous Scottisboro Case, of which an account[33] was published in 1950 by one of the men in the case. This was Haywood Patterson. He was sentenced to death no less than three times in trials which eminent American lawyers called "frame-ups," and finally sentenced to seventy-five years in prison. He escaped to write: "They transferred us to the death row at Kilby Prison ... Six cells each side and a thirteenth for a toilet. At the end of the row was the cell that held the electric chair ... July 10th came. I'll never forget that day, because they turned the juice on in the death chamber. The State of Alabama burned Will Stokes, an axe-killer. When they turned on the current for Stokes the z-z-z-z-z-z[34] of the current sounded right through the row. Then it stopped and a guard came along and said: 'Stokes died hard. They had to stick a needle through his head to make sure of it.'" A needle through the head! They might just as well have hanged him. The more one reads of electrocution, the less pleasant it seems, although in theory it is no doubt satisfying to the modern scientific mind. The fundamental mistake consists in believing that a new science can always be better than an old art. It is like comparing one of those modern soft drinks made of chemicals and artificial colouring-matter with one of those delicious old liqueurs made from a traditional recipe by experienced monks. The undiscerning modern palate favours the chemically manufactured rubbish, and has lost the sensitivity for knowing what is infinitely superior in every way.

The above opinions are quoted merely to show that, in England and elsewhere where hanging is the fashionable method of State execution, the authorities need have far less on their conscience than the unconscionable barbarians and savages who practice decapitation and electrocution. Against electrocution might also be mentioned the case of the Japanese gentleman, Jugiro, who begged the Warden of Sing Sing to have him beheaded, on the principle that of all evils he preferred what he considered to be the least.

THE ROSENBERGS

The electrocution of Julius and Ethel Rosenberg at Sing Sing in June 1953, because of the nature of their crime, the "cold war" atmosphere of the trial, and subsequent efforts to have the death sentence changed to one of life imprisonment, once again focused the attention of the world on the macabre elements in this method of execution. It showed once again that the still crude science of electrocution cannot compete with the mature art of hanging if any consideration is to be given to the feelings of onlookers, of whom ten were permitted to be present at this State killing. The executioner was Mr. Joseph Fancel, and Julius Rosenberg was the first to be dealt with. As he walked into the death chamber, witnesses noticed that the right leg of his trousers had been slit to permit the application of the electrode, and a moment later they saw the helmet containing the cathode element placed on his head, the face being masked with a dark leather covering down to the chin to avoid showing those present the expressions of death-agony. *Quelle délicatesse!* Experience proves that human beings vary enormously in their powers of resistance to electrocution, which depends upon the strength of current and not upon voltage pressure: hence, several shocks may be required to produce what medical experts can reasonably define as death, which means that doctors have to stand by with stethoscopes at the ready to apply to the victim's chest when he or she has been given one or more doses of current. Intelligent guesswork indicates when death may have taken place. Nothing could be more hygienic. Julius Rosenberg was given a *first* shock which lasted 3 seconds, a *second* lasting 57 seconds; and a *third* of 57 seconds. The appointed witnesses "saw his body strain three times against the straps holding him to the wooden chair, heard a hiss of air escaping from his lungs as current hit him as he exhaled." A doctor could duly pronounce him dead. Then came Ethel Rosenberg's turn. An eye-witness account was published in the London *Sunday Dispatch* (21/6/1953): "After the *fourth* (shock) guards removed one of the two straps and the two doctors applied their stethoscopes. But they were not satisfied that she was dead. The executioner came to them from his switchboard in a small room 10 feet from the chair. 'Want another?' he asked. The doctors nodded. Guards replaced the straps and for the fifth time electricity was applied." The heart still beating after four jolts of current! To the people of England, long accustomed to quick hanging by a beautifully simple method, all this seems unnecessarily painful both to victim and onlookers; and the newspapers commented acidulously. It certainly seems strange that a nation so advanced in science and engineering as to be able to make highly efficient H-bombs, and some excruciatingly effective poison gases, and utterly devastating compounds for chemical and bacteriological warfare, should not be able to invent something better than the crude electric chair. Perhaps it is that every country chooses the method of execution most suitable to the temperament of its people.

USA: Abolition and Caryl Chessman

The case quoted was of execution by the electric chair, a form which the superior English regard as having little to commend it. Six States in the American Union have to tally abolished capital punishment, and seem little the worse for abolition except in moral prestige. They are Wisconsin (1853), Maine (1887), Minnesota (1911), Alaska and Hawaii (before achieving statehood); and Delaware so late as 1958. Michigan, Rhode Island, and North Dakota count themselves as abolitionists because, although they retain the death penalty for treason, and for murder in jail by a murderer, they do not now invoke their power to execute. Eight other states abolished the penalty of death and later restored it: Missouri abolished in 1917 and in 1919 restored the penalty because two undesirables killed a pair of policemen in a gun-fight. On the whole execution is declining—as in Britain; and for more or less the same reasons. But if the death penalty in general is not so popular as it was in the United States, the position there is interesting because in some States the condemned person has a choice of methods of execution. Hanging holds sway in some places. In Utah they have hanging or shooting; and thirty-three States kill the redundant citizen by lethal gas or electric chair. These last are very useful for scientific progress, especially where lethal gas is used: chosen observers can look into the death chamber and see the whole convulsive reactions of the person who is being gassed. No doubt it must all be highly enlightening. Then again, the United States can keep a person *on the verge* of execution longer than any other country in the world: the democratic idea being that he or she is allowed every kind of legal loophole to escape the final arrow of outraged fortune. This was beautifully exemplified in the celebrated case of Caryl Chessman (of grade-school education, IQ 136) who spent an all-time record in Death Row. This man under sentence of death since 1948 wrote a book, *Cell 2455 Death Row*, published in 1954 and a best seller. Half a million copies sold in the United States alone and it was translated into a dozen languages, thereby providing the government with some cultural propaganda and making Chessman a world personality like the U.S. President, Khrushchev, General de Gaulle—and, one might add, Hitler. Chessman even achieved the honour of having his portrait in glorious colour by the painter Bernard Safran on the cover of *Time* (The Weekly News Magazine) and what man could desire greater fame? This is not the place to argue the merits of his case from the moral, legal, or social point of view. But one thing is quite certain: no condemned man has ever had greater publicity: it was world-wide. His case aroused the passions of pros and cons, and one of the slogans used by the cons was:

STOP INSTITUTIONALIZED MURDER!

—by which was meant killing by the State for crime. Ballads were written about this man, the equivalent of many books was

written and published about him. And, be it noted, the less famous
condemned were meanwhile all but ignored. They were neither so
articulate nor so interesting in themselves, though they were all
human beings. State Governor Brown of California, who tried
to have capital punishment abolished there, pointed out that the
other men under sentence of death were "the weak, the poor, and
the ignorant." Who ever heard of "the strong, the rich, and the
cultivated" being executed?—except, perhaps, when passions are
high, as in moments of violent revolutionary anger. Chessman was
kept on the verge of death for twelve years, it was explained by
interpreters of American justice, because of the democratic nature
of American law which gives an accused every possible opportunity
to clear himself. It did *not* occur to anybody with the necessary
power that twelve years on the verge of death is a worse punishment
than death itself. When Federal District Judge Louis Goodman
tried by telephone to order a stay of Chessman's execution for
further legal arguments, his secretary misdialled the number—no
doubt, poor woman, in her trepidation. One minute later the fatal
cyanide tablets were dropped into the can of acid under Chessman's
metal perforated commode in the death chamber. And Chessman
died. How he died you will learn in a moment.

WIDER MORAL OF THE CHESSMAN CASE

But, first, let us pause and consider whether, in a moment of awful
trepidation, some key person in the well-worked-out chain of
precautionary measures to prevent nuclear war "by an accident,"
could not fumble for a similar reason. In the Chessman case, the
life of one man was at stake. In the event of a possible nuclear war,
the lives of millions of people would be at stake. And is it in the
least unreasonable for anybody who knows how fallible the human
element can be to envisage a human failure in the most dramatic of
all moments in the history of mankind? The human mind is rarely
capable of perfect functioning in such a moment. With all due
respect to rulers and others concerned, we must *not* be expected

to believe in *their* infallibility. The very idea of such a war must be abolished, and all those terrible instruments of destruction must be eliminated from risk of the ever-fallible human element. It just is *not* safe for man to possess and control such weapons: in given circumstances *they* are capable of controlling *him*.

If there is a major moral in the death of Chessman this is it.

The Death of Chessman

The actual manner of his death was no credit to anybody. Making all allowances, the execution was efficiently carried through by those immediately responsible. It took place in an apple-green steel and glass chamber, with a number of spectators looking in at him through the glass. When the pellets were dropped into the bucket, a moment elapsed and Chessman's head jerked back and his hands clenched convulsively. The scene then all but paralyzed the spectators with horror. The victim's head rocked forward in a dreadful spasm, and again and again his body went into convulsions. This sort of horrific drama lasted for no less than *nine minutes* before the poor sufferer died—died from torture administered in the name of a public ignorant of what was really happening, and largely apathetic through ignorance.

Ugly Stain on Civilization

After this unworthy event many people not only in the U.S.A. but all over the world were wondering about the position of *homo sapiens* when such events could happen today in any country claiming to be civilized. The case evoked from the most distinguished living Brazilian lawyer—Supreme Court Justice Hungria, author of the new Civil Code of Brazil—this plea: "Caryl Chessman is the most eloquent assurance of the need to wipe out once and for all time the death penalty, *that ugly stain on civilization*." The simple fact is that the Chessman execution, and the circumstances which led up to it, brought the name of the United States of America into disrepute all over the world. The minor moral of it all is that, however crazy our lunatic governments may be about weapons of destruction and preparations for press-button nuclear and other even less attractive kinds of modern warfare, they do not enhance their own value in the public mind by indulging in such minor horrors as the asphyxiation of a midget such as this man. They merely demonstrate that they are lacking in what has been known as soul. Something must be done to put something useful and tolerable in its place, before the rottenness goes further. Hanging seems a poor and rather harmless business—and even full of good qualities—in comparison with what has happened and is likely to happen not to one person but to humanity.

Here we may well turn to something brighter! So, back to hanging!

Honours for Hangmen

I have already referred to the bad pay and lack of pension arrangements for hangmen. In view of the delicacy and importance of their work it is remarkable that they do not receive honours or decorations; not even the humble O.B.E. ever goes the way of the hangman. It is a scandal. If *we* cannot decorate them, why does not some philanthropist—an armament king, for example—offer them a prize of honour? When will there be a Nobel Prize for our hangmen, as there is for other great artists, scientists, and public benefactors? We never see even a statue erected to our executioners. An acquaintance would not believe me when I assured him that there was not in the whole of London a single statue of a hangman. Although I swore this to him he still remained in doubt: for he had inspected most of the existing statues, and his suspicions had been aroused. Nor are our most worthy executioners ever buried in Westminster Abbey. They pass and are forgotten. Even the name "hangman" is discreditable with us. In Germany they were sometimes called Master of the Gallows (*Galgenmeister*) or even a kind of judge (*Hinrichter*): until other judges objected. Supposing some great person in history were discovered to have been an executioner, in addition to the achievements for which his name is now honoured, what then? Should we continue to honour his name? If for example, it was proved by some of the higher critics that Christ, in addition to being a carpenter, had acted as public executioner, could we still reverence Him? And supposing that the economic circumstances in which He lived drove Him (as it drove our own Mr. Berry and others) to this as the only practicable means of earning a livelihood, would we admire the state of society in which He lived? Would we admire the Roman governors for employing Him?

Who Ought to be Hanged?

These questions are submitted for the consideration of the gentle reader, who will answer them in accordance with his complexes. But first of all consider this: Is there a man or woman amongst us who can honestly say that he or she does not know at least one person who ought to be hanged? As we look around our own circle of acquaintances and our public life (to say nothing of such institutions as the stock exchanges of the world), does not the purely ethical case for capital punishment seem overwhelming? When we look back at history and think of the names of hundreds of rascals who escaped the common hangman, argument becomes needless. When we think of the gala days of the past (*gala* in Anglo-Saxon meant gallows), we realize how much we are missing. A well conducted execution is like a sonnet by Petrarch, a statue by Michelangelo, or a painting by Velazquez, and would be a spectacle far more satisfying to the British public than a Shakespeare play, or even a good dog-race.

George Bernard Shaw Quoted

There are few matters of interest that have not been touched upon by that Grand Old Irishman of English letters, Mr. George Bernard

Shaw, and he does not entirely fail us on capital punishment. His final pronouncement on the subject appeared in the *Sunday Express* of 12th December, 1947. "Capital punishment is a term which indicates muddled thinking," he said, and then he went on to clarify things. What do you do with a mad dog which runs amok through the streets biting and infecting everybody it comes across? Fond as we may be of dogs, we must kill this one on the spot in the public interest. So it must be with "mischievous human beings" who are "vermin in the commonwealth." Humane treatment may act in certain cases and be necessary. But "the ungovernables, the ferocious, the conscienceless, the idiots, the self-centred myops and morons"—G.B.S. asks, "what of them?" and he answers: "Kill, kill, kill, kill, *kill* them. The most amiably soft-hearted monarch, confronted with a death warrant, must sign it or abdicate as unfit to reign." Excellent. But how are we to kill them? Here, I regret to say, Mr. Shaw let us down rather badly. He said: "Kill (the incorrigible) kindly and apologetically, if possible without consciousness on his part." Euthanasia. But wouldn't a man who was to be killed painlessly be expecting it to happen every time he fell asleep? It *sounds* all right, and I am sure that nonagenarian Shaw meant quite well, but I have heard expert opinion that there is a good chance of a person so threatened becoming insane; and it would hardly be quite fair to kill a poor lunatic, even though nobody need be made a bit the wiser about his insanity. No, Mr. Shaw, this will not do! What's *wrong* with hanging? Where is the muddled thinking? Now, although I have not the slightest doubt but that the late Herr Hitler and our contemporary General Franco would certainly agree with Mr. Shaw's "Kill, kill, kill, kill, *kill* them," they would not waste time over it. "It won't hurt at all," say our hangmen to their clients. And they know far more about it than ever Mr. Shaw did. A much more reasonable attitude is that of a good Christian who writes as follows: "The reason why the death penalty should not be abolished is because it is the Law of God (Genesis ix, 6). We in this country are more responsible than any other nation, because we have the open Bible with all God's commandments and laws written therein; and we keep or break them, for our blessing if we obey them, and are cursed if we disobey them. God has not changed His laws or commandments since the time He gave them—'*I am the Lord, I change not.*' He has plainly shown us that there are two breeds in this world: children of God and children of the Devil ..." I need not quote further, for all this writer's argument amounts to comes more or less to the same as that of Mr. George Bernard Shaw, and it adds up that the children of God should kill the children of the Devil— Q.E.D. and R.I.P. Incidentally the correspondent I have quoted says that when the Lord returns to this world He will see that all His Laws are kept—and that means that, if we should ever be such unbelievers as to abolish hanging in Britain, the good Lord Himself will reimpose the death penalty. Parliament, please note.

PROFESSOR DR. JOAD, WIT AND PHILOSOPHER

Then there are the views of the late Dr. Joad. Dr. Cyril Edwin Mitchinson Joad, everybody knows, was a great philosopher of our time—and an essentially English one at that. We ignore the opinion of such a philosopher at the risk of social embarrassment. Professor[35] Dr. Joad had long been writing a column of his philosophy for the *Sunday Dispatch*, an admirable weekly newspaper which serialized *Forever Amber* and since then has serialized the sexo-sadistic *Flesh of the Orchid* by that master of this branch of literature, Mr. James Hadley Chase. And many other masterpieces written by very clever geniuses of our time. Naturally this organ supports the Conservative-Imperialist cause. In reply to a question (from one of his thousands of correspondents) asking for his view on the proposal to abolish the death penalty, the great philosopher Joad replied: "I favour its retention on humanitarian grounds," and, warming to his subject he said: "The objection to the death penalty is a piece of canting sentimentality arising, I suppose, from belief to the effect that human life is sacred and should not be taken." The objection is cant, the Professor explained, cant from a most destructive generation which has killed more than 20,000,000 human beings in two wars and is now devoting big money and the best brains to the preparation of more efficient means of destruction. One can hardly restrain a cheer at such robust common sense. There is far too much cant, rant, and fustian in contemporary discussion of capital punishment. Hangmen in gratitude should pass round the hat for all this, and I am not sure that guillotiners, electrocutioners, garotters, gasmen, headsmen, and other ranks of State executioners would object to offering a small contribution as a token of their appreciation for as fine a piece of philosophy as has been produced by a true Englishman since Hobbes wrote his masterly *Leviathan*, the work which provided a philosophic blue-print for the totalitarian super-State. A word of warning is, however, necessary; and it is offered in the most kindly spirit. Many of us who have hanging at heart feel that in moments of extreme creative exuberance Dr. Joad tended somewhat to confuse issues and to end up by leaving his readers bewildered; or, which is much more amusing, by saying precisely nothing in a very laughable way. Unkind people have been heard to say that he deserved to be hanged for some of his witticisms, one logician of my acquaintance adding, "*and* drawn *and* quartered"! One must not take such people too seriously. Another school of thought on the subject might be described as having the same view as Dr. Blunt (Anglican Bishop of Bradford) has on the virgin birth: "It is not easily believed; but it is merely presumption or prejudice which will easily reject it."

THE GREAT NUREMBERG HANGINGS

Forever memorable in the proud annals of execution will be the Great Hangings at Nuremberg in the Year of Grace 1946. Eleven leaders of the Nazi movement who had been tried for war crimes and crimes against humanity sat down one October evening (23rd) to their Last Supper of canned American-German sausage and cold cuts with potato salad, bread, and tea. The same evening the cinema of the Court of Justice announced next day's screen attraction, which had been well chosen for the occasion. It was *Deadline for Murder*. Everything about the Nuremberg trials was excellent until they came to the great problem of what form of execution was to be used. Needless to say, hanging won—as every sensible person thought it would. Now comes a very terrible story, one which causes my inanimate typewriter to tremble with indignation as I slowly and hesitatingly tap it out. Instead of appointing an English hangman, they appointed an American! Woe, woe, *woe* that such a monumental international insult should be possible! And in the twentieth century, too, when good and polite international behaviour has progressed so far. I will not, I cannot dwell on the lack of tact, the lack of good sense, the lack of common decency shown by passing over in this way the unchallengeable claims of British hangmen to this high honour. A Britain weakened to the point of exhaustion in two World Wars had to yield to American insistence that the kudos for hanging those awful Nazis should be American. The Americans love to be loved, and wished to have the kudos for the final act of justice. As we shall see in a moment, it proved to be a grave mistake from many points of view, not least of which was that of style. So great an event in the annals of execution ought to have redounded to the credit of hanging, this being the method of killing chosen and accepted by all parties interested— apart from some of the Nazis, who would have preferred shooting. I have no racial or anti-American feelings; nor any personal grudge against the decent man chosen to execute the awful Nazis. He was U.S.A. Army Master-Sergeant John C. Woods (43), of San Antonio, who, in his fifteen years as U.S. Army executioner, had honestly hanged 347 of his fellows. His record was excellent. Said he afterwards: "I hanged those ten Nazis"—Marshal Goering dodged the event by poisoning himself—"and I am proud of it. I wasn't nervous. A fellow can't afford to have nerves in this business. I want to put in a good word for those G.I.s who helped me. I am trying to get them a promotion. The way I look at this hanging job, somebody has to do it. I got into it kind of by accident, years ago in the States." This hanging job! Do you not notice a certain vulgarity about all of this statement? "This business," indeed, as if it were just a matter of filthy lucre! One would almost think he was talking of stockbroking or something of that sort, and not of a great art. Then again you will notice that he "got into it kind of by accident." By accident forsooth! Does not one's blood boil to read of such things about this essential work, which must never be far away from any order. The weekly *Time* (28/10/1946) published a good account of the Great Hangings at Nuremberg, but it fell to the *London Star* veteran crime reporter and expert on hangings to make known some of the appalling truth. Mr. Cecil Catling of the *Star* was not the only reporter to declare that the executions had been cruelly bungled—his first-hand evidence is in part confirmed by a French report. Reporter Catling declared that there was not enough room for the men to drop, which would mean that their necks had not been properly broken and that they must have died of slow strangulation. In addition, he said that they were not properly tied, so that some hit the platform with their heads as they went down and their noses were torn off.

Defence of a Choice Hangman

The United States Army flatly denied Mr. Catling's objective interpretation. The flat denial fell flat in Britain, where Mr. Catling's integrity as a reporter and experienced eye-witness of hangmanship was unchallenged. He was a man who had never been known to grind an axe and all his life he had been witnessing the quick, artistic work of Britain's hangmen. The Nuremberg fiasco must have shocked him deeply. Now we come to the syndicated French report, which I quote from *Le Patriote* (24/10/1947) of Toulouse. When it was suggested to him by the French reporter that the men hanged had taken an "abnormal" time to die, that they died from strangulation and not from broken necks, and that in the drop they had hit the trap, Master-Sergeant Woods replied with dignity, "The only people capable of disseminating such information are manifestly amateurs who know nothing about it"—I translate from the French—"If you doubt my word, ask the Medical Corps. The medical officer present at the execution said to me immediately afterwards, 'You have not bungled a single one'—he referred to the fact that the necks of the condemned men had been broken in their drop. As regards suffocation, my clients emitted certain sounds and made certain movements after their drop; according to the doctor's opinion it is merely a question of reflexes." Rubbish! This is always due to a lack of style in the hangmanship. Master-Sergeant Woods was clearly a well-educated man, and an honest one, too, for when cross-examined about the trap being hit, he said that the hanged man would know "nothing about it," and as for blood found on the faces afterwards, he said: "*That is quite natural*—it happens when the condemned opens his mouth at the moment of the drop and bites his tongue. He knows nothing about it. *It is a thing which might happen in the course of any execution, however perfect it might be.*" Very interesting, very humane, and, no doubt, very true. But it is all most inartistic in the English sense of hanging, and that is perhaps the most serious criticism that can be made without damage to the cause and purpose of hanging, though some of the frank and honest American's disclosures were, to say the least, tactless by English—well, perhaps more hypocritical standards. I am glad to be able to clear this hangman's name of sordid suspicions on the part of the ignorant, and of vile accusations on the part of the malicious. Were not the ten men hanged, and did they not die from hanging? So why introduce subtleties about strangulation or neck-breaking or trifles about hitting the trap or bleeding? Irrelevant and absurd! Master-Sergeant Woods concluded: "They are my last clients, I've had a bellyful of it" (*j'en ai assez*, in the words of the French interviewer, a bowdlerization of *j'en ai plein le cul*). "Have you seen the British specialist in hanging who has hanged so many people? Why, his work has made an old man of him. He is all broken up and one gets the impression that his head and hands are about to fall off. That is the result of the terrible nervous tension to which the hangman is subjected." The name of the "British specialist in hanging" is given—it is a household word in Britain—but, of course, delicacy prevents me from repeating it. Besides, Woods' statement may well be untrue and/or libellous, for I think that Britain's national hangmen are made of sterner stuff than one gathers from this remark. Those whom I have had the honour to meet were fine healthy men with no signs of nervous wear and tear. Woods added that he always carried a couple of revolvers for self-defence, and that he could hit a bull's-eye shooting from both hands. How many British hangmen can say that? Happily they do not need any sort of defence—except, of course, when they travel to Ireland or go abroad. Less civilized peoples do not have the same profound regard for public executioners as law-abiding British have for their worthy hangmen. But security precautions have to be taken when alien circumstances require them.

A brief postscript has to be written to the Great Nuremberg Hangings.

Master-Sergeant John Woods, to quote the words of a news-message from Boise, Idaho, dated 26/7/1950, "*met his death on a special assignment for the United States Government.*" So ended gloriously the life of the man who knew the closest details of the Nuremberg hangings. In this way ended what reliable evidence indicates to have been that kind of artistic failure which serious critics of hangmanship must always regard from first to last as a classic bungling, a masterpiece of ineptitude, and, some think, based upon a breach of a fundamental principle of jurisprudence; though we need not worry about this last. It is hanging with which we are concerned, and Nuremberg brought it into disrepute. But only for a moment. From Nuremberg onwards the British had their full say in hanging Nazi war criminals and the fine British hangmaster Albert Pierrepoint stepped forward to restore confidence. He did not bungle anything that we know of, for the British are masters of the fine art of concealing or explaining or ignoring their errors, when such there be. It is to be hoped that the lesson will not be lost on the brash Americans. If there are any more international hangings to be done, they should be left entirely to the more sensitive British. There are some things which the Americans can *not* teach them; and of these the fine art of hanging is one of the most important.

THE EXECUTIONER WHO WORKS FROM A DESK

Of Adolf Eichmann and the holocaust of murder of which he was organizer—an executioner sitting at a desk and working with card indexes, files, secretaries, clerks, and all the office amenities which Germany could provide—it is not necessary to say much. He was a worshipper of power and authority, sheltering behind both, and finding cathartic expression in obeying Hitler's orders for what was called "The Final Solution of the Jewish Problem." By this was meant the total elimination of Jews from all territory occupied by the Germans during the Second World War. In those territories there were 6,382,000 Jews in 1933, today (1961) there are 746,500. The Nazis are known to have liquidated some six million of them. This is the most horrific instance of mass-execution—amounting to genocide—of which there is anything approaching a close record in human history. The Nuremberg trials and Eichmann's own trial exposed the horrors perpetrated by the Nazis; and there is no need to dwell on them here. In spite of the magnitude of his executions, Eichmann failed in his main purpose: Jews survived to try him. To execute him could not bring back any of his unfortunate victims. Nor will it prevent some other power-fiend, who finds circumstances favourable, from repeating the crime of genocide, should this seem desirable in the interests of political expediency. This is perhaps the saddest part of the story: the fact that humanity is quite unable to learn from experience in matters of power-struggles. It is written of Eichmann that he had "a mysterious attraction for some women" and that "unanimously they found him polite, considerate, and filled with a romantic melancholy." No doubt. This was the efficient humanitarian who, on orders from Himmler, and finding that Zyklon-B gas killed painlessly (after a successful experiment on 600 Russian prisoners of war), decided that this gentle and easy form of death was the "humane method" for which he was searching. The same gas had been suggested by American experience. Whereupon he ordered the building of chambers for gassing 9,000 human beings in a working day, with nearby the crematoria necessary for the disposal of their last bodily remains. Eichmann was what the Germans aptly call *kadavergehorsam*, which may be literally translated as "corpse-obedient": that is, endowed with that supreme quality of obedience which will enable even a corpse to do exactly what it is told. It is this quality which makes the Germans so dangerous, as those of us who are old enough remember from two World Wars. Hitler gave the orders; and Eichmann obeyed. If this story of Eichmann points any moral, it is the danger of power-worship and of blind obedience to a political master. And also that the executioner who works bureaucratically, sitting comfortably at a desk, merely obeying orders from above, is the sophisticated or advanced stage in the evolution of executioners, in comparison with which that of our simple-hearted hangmen is merely primitive. Does it not make England feel proud of her honest-to-god hangmen?

ANTI-HANGING CAMPAIGNS

Those of us who have at heart the interests of hangmen can never forget the awful trepidation with which we read the recommendations of a Royal Commission which, in that terrible year 1930, had thoroughly investigated the whole question of capital punishment. It actually recommended the abolition of the death penalty for a "trial" period of five years! And would you believe it, there was not one word of sympathy or any consideration for the hangmen of Britain in that bulky volume of pro and con evidence and testimony. One sees, of course, that the Commission came to the conclusion that it would be "safe" to try abolition; caution demanded that it be for a set period. For five years only. Then it could be reconsidered in the light of experience. Many of us felt at long last that

This royal throne of kings, this sceptr'd isle ...
This precious stone set in the silver sea ...
This blessed plot, this earth, this realm, this England

was about to lose its grip on an institution which we have inherited from our furthest and noblest ancestry. And not only our Anglo-Saxon ancestry, because capital punishment dates from that wonderful code of Hammurabi, 2285–2242 B.C., the oldest known code of laws in the world, venerated by everybody who has respect for law and order. And now, in Britain, there was this sinister threat to a great and noble public institution which represents one of the most beautiful and harmonious of all the fine arts. Hanging in the balance! The lawyers shook their heads; the bishops fingered the gold crosses on their watch-chains; the public hangmen puffed hard at their pipes; and potential murderers threw their caps in the air—or so it was said at the time by law-abiding rentiers of Kensington Gore and many other places, some of them outside of England because of gout and taxation. But time passed and the true strength of the breed asserted itself. In other words, nothing happened. Once again the hangmen of England were able to breathe freely, to enjoy again the full flavour of their mild-and-bitter beer. A long and stubborn campaign by the abolitionists was thwarted, frustrated, and happily brought to nothing by the sound common sense of the Conservatives then in power. Wait! Do not imagine that those defeated abolitionists took it lying down, for one must never forget that they, too, are English, just as English as the others. In true English fashion they took their defeat as Englishmen generally do, and merely regarded it as an experience from which useful lessons could be drawn. Hitler—and many another before him—learnt to his cost that Englishmen are not unduly alarmed about losing a battle, so long as it is not the last battle. And so it was that the campaigners against hanging got going again, and the year 1948 saw the threat against hangmen dangling right over their heads, so to speak, like one of their own ropes on execution morning, and ready to suspend *them*. Hangmen came to be in greater danger than ever.

The anti-hanging campaigners were as lively as they had ever been, and they had gained some notable supporters, one of the most important being no other personage than Lord Templewood, perhaps better known as Sir Samuel Hoare.

LORD TEMPLEWOOD ON HANGING

Sam picked up his musket and rushed into the fray with an article in the *Evening Standard* of 26th November, 1947. He said many interesting things about hanging, with which as ex-Home Secretary—and a very humane one—he was thoroughly acquainted. Here are some extracts from an article which can only be regarded as a stab in the back for the whole corps of public executioners:

> "It is urged ... that the death penalty, although it is seldom carried into effect, acts as a power in reserve to deter criminals from murder. It is further claimed that, if there were no death penalty, burglars would more often carry arms and be more ready to kill their victims in order to avoid discovery. It is not possible either to prove or disprove these arguments, except to say that, when there were 250 capital offences, crimes of robbery and violence were far more common than they are today. I can only state my own view founded upon my experience as Home Secretary. It is that most murderers do not seem to be influenced by the fear of hanging when they commit their crimes. A high percentage of the murders known to the police are committed by the insane, and most of the others are the results of fits of passion ... The death penalty is an act of despair. The majority of murderers are not hardened criminals. Many of them are first-offenders, and there is a considerable body of evidence to be had from prison officials to the effect that, where murderers

are reprieved and subsequently released, they usually
make good. Secondly, I am convinced that executions
place an intolerable strain upon many prison governors
and officers. It is not sufficiently realized that the men
and women who now enter the Prison Service rightly
regard themselves as social workers with a definite
vocation. To many of them an execution, with all
its grim surroundings, is the very negation of their
devoted work. An execution demoralizes the life of a
prison for weeks, besides creating the worst kind of
morbid excitement outside the prison walls. Lastly, I
do not consider that the State should in peacetime take
human life ... The more I have heard in recent years
of the terrible number of executions on the Continent,
the more deeply I have felt that it is the duty of the
British Government to show by the abolition of the
death penalty its refusal to fall back upon an antiquated
lex talionis and itself take human life. For these reasons,
I consider that the abolition of capital punishment
should be included in the Criminal Justice Bill, and
that there should be no such compromises as a period
of experiment or the grading of murder."

April 1948: House of Commons *Against* Hanging!

Things warmed up in this campaign to a point at which the
then (Labour) Government decided that something would really
have to be done about hanging. The position was an extremely
difficult one for any government, and for reasons not without
interest. Hanging just then somewhat resembled Franco's Spain
in English politics: members of the Government very honestly
did not like it, and would be glad never to hear it mentioned.
Would they now live up to all their earlier Socialist enthusiasms
and take the lead in the abolition of capital punishment in
Britain? No, certainly not! And, pray why not? Answer: because

it would be *politically* inopportune—that is, it might lose votes when the Government had to go to the country. In January 1927 the Labour Party in Britain had put out a strong "Manifesto on Capital punishment" in which abolition was advocated. That Manifesto was signed by twenty-seven prominent Labour politicians, a few of whom had become Cabinet Ministers in the 1945 Labour Government—for example Ernest Bevin, Creech Jones, F.W. Jowett, K.C., and Herbert Morrison. Mr. Chuter Ede, before he became Home Secretary, was also a life-long abolitionist. What were all these people to do if it came to a vote in the House of Commons? And it did reach that point on the 14th of April, 1948, after long debates on the new Criminal Justice Bill.

In a free vote of the House of Commons 245 Members voted for the abolition of capital punishment and 222 voted in favour of retention.

HOUSE OF LORDS TO THE RESCUE

No less than forty-three Labour Ministers *abstained* from voting! Among those who abstained were humanitarians such as the Law Officers of the Crown, and Stafford Cripps and Mr. Aneurin Bevan—the latter a politician who showed such promise that many people even then regarded him as a future Prime Minister, another Welsh Wizard. Although there had long been agitation and campaigning against hanging, this was the first occasion in the history of Britain that a House of Commons had *voted* against the death penalty. But even so, the hangmen had no need to tremble for their office. There was still the House of Lords to be reckoned with, and that formidable old body quickly showed that it was in traditional good form. The Lords refused to accept the decision of the House of Commons and they erased from the Bill the clause which suspended the death penalty—on 1st June of that same year 1948. The atmosphere of the Upper Chamber was at times that of 1810, when Chief Justice Lord Ellenborough opposed the abolition of the death penalty for stealing to the value of a few shillings and told Their Lordships Spiritual and Temporal that if hanging for such a crime were abolished, "We shall not know whether we are on our heads or on our feet!" Merely to listen to some of those eminent men speak against the abolition of hanging enabled one to feel assured that the death penalty ran no great risk of total abolition in Britain. Here are extracts from the great speeches:

> "I for one, do not feel inclined to take part in an experiment which may be at the expense of the lives of every policeman and every warder in the country."—*Lord Schuster* (27/4/48).
>
> "I think there will be a good deal to be said ... for enlarging the possible application of that penalty (of death) for a five-year period at this time of unusual unsettlement and disturbance." "It is a great evil to put a man to death, but to erase the death penalty from the statute book might be a greater evil still."—*Bishop of Truro* (28/4/48).
>
> "If this Bill goes through in its present form, it cannot be said that Parliament rates human life very highly."— *Lord Llewellyn* (1/6/48).
>
> "Who are the people you are going to expose to this experiment? Not, I dare say, those of us who live in security, but the mass of the people of this country— women who at this hour fear, as they never feared before, the knock on the door after it is dark, and who have some reason to fear it ..."—*Lord Simon* (2/6/48).
>
> "This clause is not yet law; it may never be law—I certainly hope it will never be law." —*Another Lord.*
>
> "Is it a safe time or a proper time to carry out an experiment which must mean gambling with the lives of the people?"—*Lord Goddard, Lord Chief Justice* (2/6/48).

Et patati, et patata.

JUDICIAL PSYCHOLOGY

It is possible that some readers will be surprised to hear that judges are so adamant about hanging, but there is nothing new in this. In the edition of the famous Newgate Calendar, with an introduction by that distinguished lawyer Sir Norman Birkett[36] (Folio Society, 1951), he reminds us that until 1826 the punishment for every felony in Britain was death; that in 1748 a boy of ten was sentenced to death; and that this sentence was *unanimously approved by the whole body of judges* "in justice to the public." Also, that a woman who murdered her husband was guilty of "Petit Treason" and sentenced to be burned alive, "though frequently strangled into unconsciousness first" (no doubt a humanitarian impulse); and that even in those days there was a school of thought which protested against the growing leniency of the Criminal Code and—in the same way as many today clamour for more hangings and floggings—clamoured for something "lingering with boiling oil or molten lead in it" to make delinquents have respect for the law. It would appear from a panoramic view of judicial mentality, from early times to the present, that most good judges are strongly opposed to any relaxation in the law which might deprive the public of a legal right to sadistic enjoyment. No doubt this is sound judicial psychology. We all know that there can be arguments in favour of a retention of the death penalty in certain circumstances. For example, if States must have wars, they must also see that those who fight their battles do not run away at critical moments when the enemy has to be faced. Hence, the military mind usually offers the soldier the *certainty* of being executed by his own side if he should run away, against the *possibility* that he will come out of battle alive if he takes his chance with his comrades. And, if it be conceded that war is a reasonable activity, such an argument is not un reasonable—even allowing for the fact that it might indicate some lack of confidence in his men on the part of the commander. But that is a war risk which must be taken. And in war almost anything that is likely to help the cause is permissible. Morality can safely be left to the moralists. As for hanging murderers in time of peace, there is a school of thought which holds by its deterrent effects—we must be frightened into virtue—and another which regards it as an expression of "society's abhorrence of the crime of murder," as Lord Goddard once said, an argument not very sound but still an argument. Lord Goddard was Lord Chief Justice when the vote was taken in the House of Lords. When he gave evidence before a Royal Commission which heard evidence on the subject of hanging, he showed a vigorous support for the art. A progressive weekly, *The New Statesman and Nation* (29/4/1950), tells us this:

> In discussing with the Commission the Chalk Pit Murder Case, at which he had presided, Lord Goddard went even further. Ley, the murderer, was quite mad and a victim of a paranoiac delusion: he believed that his elderly mistress was having sexual relations with the young barman whom he murdered, although she had not the slightest acquaintance with the boy. Ley was so mad that he refused to plead insanity, and so never came up against the McNaghten formula (defining legal insanity). After the Lord Chief Justice had sentenced him to death, he was certified insane by the Home Office panel of doctors and removed to Broadmoor (Criminal Lunatic Institution), where he died within six weeks. "I suppose you would not have wished that man to hang?" Lord Goddard was asked. "I should have thought it was very proper that he should have been hanged," came the reply. It might have been proper, but it would have been a breach of the Common Law of England.

The long and short of it is that, when in doubt—*hang*. And that, so far as one could gather from the debates in the House of Lords, seemed to be the opinion of the flower of Britain. There must be no compromise, no further concessions, not even when—as had happened—the elected representatives of the people in a free vote in the Commons decided on abolition. The hangmen of England once again had their minds put at ease behind the great authority of the Lords Spiritual and Temporal. Is not this a powerful argument in favour of the hereditary Chamber of Legislators? Every hangman thinks that it is.

HANGING IN SUSPENSE

Hanging was saved by the noble Lords, but still the fact remained that the Commons had voted for the abolition and for a time executions ceased. Now hanging could safely be resumed; and it was. Yet the position was unsatisfactory. The politicians were thinking of votes at the next General Election, and it seemed desirable that, if the unpleasant business could not be hushed up and put away with other skeletons in the political cupboard, something must be done to quieten the noisy abolitionists. Britain excels all other countries in the world in the art of dealing with unpleasant problems so that the faces of those in authority are saved in such a way that criticism is silenced. There are many ways of doing this, one of which is to appoint a Royal Commission with terms of reference which will enable an inquiry to be drawn out almost as long as is desirable: and then neatly shelved if the Commission's conclusions do not suit the political requirements of the moment. A few months after the Lords had rejected the decision of the Commons to abolish the death penalty in Britain, the Labour Government in 1949 appointed a Royal Commission. The terms of reference were to inquire whether "capital punishment for murder should be limited or modified"—not whether it should be *abolished*, which was the real question at issue between Lords and Commons.

To make sure that there should be no nonsense, Prime Minister Attlee declared that the Commission *would not be allowed to recommend total abolition*. So, once again, *whatever might happen, hanging would be saved in the process of political face-saving.*

It seemed fairly certain that, with these intelligent measures for the security of hanging, much water would run under the bridges before the question could again become a nuisance to Labour or other politicians. The only serious challenge to hanging could come from the House of Commons, which again might vote in favour of abolition. The Lords could always be relied upon to quash any untoward exuberance in the Lower House in favour of abolition. And then, when a decent time had elapsed, there could always be another Royal Commission, with well-worded terms of reference. If the Conservatives should defeat Labour at a General Election, hanging would be so secure from assault that even a Royal Commission would not be necessary. For a moment hanging was in suspense in Britain. That dangerous moment passed. In the happy year 1951 Britain was back where she started before the House of Commons "shocked the whole country with its vote in favour of abolition," as a great Conservative newspaper put it. The national conscience need not be unduly perturbed by this minor question at a time when far greater things were on the horizon. The gallows would be there to play its part in the battle for human rights. "Depend upon it," said Dr. Johnson, "when a man knows that he is to be hanged in a fortnight, it concentrates his mind wonderfully."

POST-WAR CRIMES—THE CAUSE

Constant readers of the admirable daily Press (not excluding the equally admirable sabbath newspapers, some of which have a true sense of moral and other values) have noticed that, after the end of World War II, there was an increase in crimes of violence everywhere—as there was after World War I and, indeed, as there is everywhere after a good war. It need hardly surprise any sensible person that, when healthy young men have been trained and brain-washed to be ferocious (or "conditioned," as the jargon has it) and to maim or, better still, kill the enemy, they bring back with them to civil life some of those very uncivil habits. One of the most important aspects of their training is to create in them a frame of mind that they must do or die and have no regard for the consequences; that, if they make a good job of the killing when circumstances are difficult, and when it is really vital to success, they may even be rewarded by gracious decorations, or achieve preferment in their unit, or—though this does not always apply— be remembered for their good work when they return home in the piping days of peace. Must not one admit that among many young men both the repugnance to taking life and the fear of losing it can be thoroughly eliminated by a sound military education? Is it any wonder, then, that in some moment of crisis in their private lives they forget their civil obligations and remember only the killing part of their governmental education? One thing seems to be dead certain: the fact that they are likely to be executed for a murder does not matter a hoot one way or the other. They have been conditioned to risk death. Although it may be entirely against the general principles expounded in this treatise, it seems necessary to put in a special plea on behalf of these unfortunate young men— unfortunate in the sense that too often the State is responsible in the first instance for their irresponsible civil conduct. I put forward this plea, well knowing that it is against the interests of hangmen and may well be dismissed as a piece of sentimental nonsense on my part. My reply is that in time of peace we should make allowances for our defenders, for whom nothing is too good in time of war.

U.S.S.R.—DEATH PENALTY ABOLISHED!

At this point a few words must be said about the U.S.S.R., a country which seems to have forced its way into the news in recent years. We cannot entirely ignore the Soviet Union nowadays. The democratic world was *flabbergasted* by the Kremlin Decree of 26th May, 1947, which: (1) abolished in peace-time the death penalty envisaged for crimes under Soviet Union laws; (2) substituted twenty-five years' "confinement in reformatory labour camps" for crimes hitherto punishable by death, and (3) replaced the death penalty by twenty-five years' "reformatory confinement" in the case of those then under sentence of death. Note that this Decree was introduced by Stalin. It was not only democrats who were flabbergasted when the

Decree was published abroad. The people who were most shaken by it were our Friends of the Gallows, for they saw immediately that this might well prove to be an exceedingly bad example. They saw as a consequence the possible disappearance from Merrie England of the rope which holds together the substance of law and order, the relegation to an undeserved obscurity of such public-spirited men as Mr. Hangman Pierrepoint, then landlord (when not O.H.M.S.) of the well-named public house "Help the Poor Struggler" at Oldham,[37] near Manchester, and immortalized by his perfect work in the SEVENTEEN HANGINGS IN ONE DAY of those bad men of Belsen and blond beastess Irma Grese. There was about this last episode one piece of unpleasantness which deserves mention here. You will hardly believe it, but the Government beat down Albert Pierrepoint about the fee for this important piece of work! Instead of the usual fifteen guineas per drop, they offered him a *lump sum* for the seventeen necks to be broken! This characteristic piece of governmental cheeseparing the poor man accepted with the characteristic philosophy of our good hangmen, though the *Sunday Pictorial* (16/9/1946), in a masterly biographical sketch and pen-portrait, records that Albert considered it to be a "tidy enough sum." To return to Russia, the worst feature of abolition of capital punishment in that country proved to be some of the things well-known Russians said about it. Mr. A.Y. Vyshinsky, for example, went so far as to state this in writing: "It is with profound satisfaction that the Soviet people will welcome this great act of *Socialist humanism*"—my italics. Socialist humanism! Many may remember that Comrade Andrei Vyshinsky was the principal prosecutor at the Moscow political trials of 1938, but they may have forgotten his eloquence at those trials. In his well-modulated voice he yelled at the judges: "Let your sentence, Comrade Judges, resound as a bell calling for new victories! Crush the accursed vipers … foul dogs ... disgusting villains! We cannot leave such people alive. They can do such things in America—where Al Capone remains alive—but not here. Thank God, Russia is not America!" Political philosophers will immediately observe that for Mr. Vyshinsky to perform the somersault does not impair the validity of "Socialist humanism," which has not changed. This humanism (and Vyshinsky's principles) can at any time be modulated in accordance with the best doctrines of Marxist-Leninist-Stalinism, a fundamental of which is that application of the doctrines be in accordance with the needs of the moment. It has been noted that the English Conservative, Lord Templewood, and the English Socialist leader, Mr. Chuter Ede, when in office opportunely modulated their views on capital punishment. Why should not Mr. Vyshinsky? So much for Soviet opinion, and one need only add that in 1950 they reintroduced capital punishment in Russia as a measure of Socialist humanism for dealing with certain purely political crimes: but not for murder.

SOVIET DECREE OF MAY 1961

In 1950, crimes of espionage, treason, and diversion (from current political dogma) were liable to capital punishment, but, in 1954, wilful murder in vile circumstances was added to the list. Since 1947 the maximum punishment for murder had been varied in accordance with the effect of reforming treatment on the person confined in a labour camp. But in May 1961, a Decree of the Supreme Soviet legislated to provide death by shooting for a variety of offences against public (that is, State) property, and for criminals who terrorized fellow-prisoners. Writing in *Izvestia*, Roman Rudenko, Prosecutor-General, said that the object of this Decree was "to prevent, sharply curtail, and finally to eradicate crime from our country"—the law had been inadequate to deal with private speculators, plunderers and parasites, and hooliganism including that perpetrated by their *stalyagi* or, as we would call them, "Teddy-boys": youngsters who dress up, have very special hair-dos, and often bash our harmless and/or helpless people for no apparent reason except perhaps out of boyish exuberance or mere playfulness. Russia is a strange country, as many have observed. Before the October Revolution of 1917 the Tsarist régime was far more sparing of the death penalty than were the more democratic governments of Britain: very high treason and attempts to kill the Tsar or members of his family were the only capital crimes. In Dostoevski's time, and later in moments of political tension, sentence of death was passed on those deemed to be dangerous political offenders: that is, those whose activities threatened or could threaten the very existence of the régime. Has not Dostoevski, who was himself sentenced to death and dragged to the place of execution, allegedly for one of these offences, written poignantly of capital punishment? And was he not terribly prejudiced against it from the morning of his last-moment reprieve? It is historically true of Russia that in that country there has long been—and consistently, except for political crimes at given moments—both public hostility and governmental reluctance in regard to inflicting the penalty of death. After the 1917 Revolution, during the period when the new Soviet régime was fighting for its existence against enemies at home and abroad, the number of capital crimes increased to almost one-third the number of crimes for which a person could be executed in calm and prosperous England of the early nineteenth century. That is, at one moment there were about seventy capital crimes in the U.S.S.R.—all of them political—as against some two hundred and twenty capital crimes in the England of the early nineteenth century—most of these against property. We have to view the subject objectively: for no country is entirely immune from either praise or criticism. Only one thing need be added here: the host of major speculators which emerged in the never-had-it-so-good Britain, when the country was liberated by Conservative rule in the 1950s, have lucky stars to thank that we have no hanging laws here like that shooting Soviet Decree of 1961. By it Russia's speculators and suchlike tended to become shot, *sans cérémonie*: they were not even provided with the formal and dignified method of execution of which we are so proud in England.

ROMAN CATHOLICS AND STATE KILLING

We may now proceed to consider another important point of view: the Roman Catholic. The English *Catholic Herald*'s Editor, in reply to a secular letter in which the correspondent said that Catholics had been "'inhibited' from taking part in anti-hanging activities" because their outlook invariably hinges on the denial of a principle which every Catholic accepts, *viz.* the right invested in the State to inflict death where sufficiently grievous crime exists, wrote[38] as follows: "We do not think ... that they (the Catholics) need have the smallest difficulty, in principle, in supporting the abolition of the death penalty." There were many other subversive suggestions in that dangerous letter, of which this may be quoted: "In a modern age where punishment is supposed to be corrective is not the continued retention of this engine of retribution an acknowledgment that society has failed?" Add this to the Soviet decision—"reformatory detention" to replace execution—and think it over. The implications which spring to mind are appalling, for one might easily draw the abominable conclusion that society has succeeded in Russia and failed in Britain: a *reductio ad absurdum*, if ever there was one. We cannot have this sort of thing, even from the editor of so democratic and liberal an organ of public opinion as the *Catholic Herald*. In the very Catholic Republic of Ireland, the Minister for Lands admitted in a debate (1952) on capital punishment that "important moral issues were involved" but that there was no alternative to the death penalty; thereupon another Catholic member of the *Dail* said that if they must have capital punishment, let execution be by the electric chair, "as hanging was cruel, brutal, and unchristian." Yet he failed to add what might have been the strongest of Irish arguments: that hanging was not merely un-Irish but was, in fact, English! There is something wrong somewhere, and I trust that all good Catholics will write to His Holiness the Pope asking for his guidance on this knotty subject. One can hardly doubt what His Holiness will say, for has he not blessed General Franco and his Falangist régime? And has not Franco achieved a high place—which he continues to hold as these lines are written—among the great executioners of history? One remembers the 30,000 republicans which El Caudillo executed during the first month after his glorious liberation of Madrid. One may, I think, take it for granted that the Pope can be relied upon to be quite sound on all matters of faith and morals; and hanging is certainly a matter of both faith *and* morals, as history has shown. Whatever the *morals* of it may be—and they are not in great doubt—we must never allow *faith* to be shaken. Besides, the world is in a state of flux, and for a State to abolish the death penalty would indicate an official confidence which might not be justifiable to established authority. At the time of the Chessman execution (on 2nd May, 1960), the editor of the *Osservatore Romano* (which, as you know, is the official organ of the Vatican) came out bluntly and wrote: "*The execution of criminals is repugnant to the modern conscience.*" This is the point of view of the majority in the anti-capital punishment camp, and long has been. Pope John XXIII may be supposed to be the inspiration behind what can only be regarded as a fundamental change in Vatican attitude in regard to this matter of State execution for crimes.

Note on Hanging, Drawing and Quartering

The delectable threefold ceremony of hanging, drawing and quartering was invented by the English, as might be expected, and was first practiced in the Year of Grace 1241. It was generally reserved for those found guilty of high treason, although, by way of diversion, it was used in other cases. Those who protested against this punishment were silenced by two sound arguments: (1) the legal and (2) the religious. Divine authority was easily found in support of the religious argument, and Coke, one of the greatest English jurists, produced a Biblical quotation to justify each part of the great ceremony (in which castration often preceded the disembowelling). The form of sentence by His Majesty's judges was as follows:

> That the traitor be dragged along the surface of the ground, tied to the tail of a horse and drawn to the gallows, and there hanged by the neck until he be half dead and then cut down; and his entrails be cut out of

his body and burnt by the executioner; then his head is
to be cut off, his body to be divided into quarters, and
afterwards his head and quarters to be set up in some
open places directed.[39]

Two points must here be noted. First, that hanging took the
place of an anaesthetic so that the drawing and quartering should
be humane. Second, that the full ceremony was reserved for those
found guilty of such un-English activities as treason and they
were nearly always people highly placed in the social scale. Simple
hanging was reserved for the proletarians and low-downs: thieves,
murderers, and the rag-tag and bob-tail element of the population.

I must not fail to mention that it is only in regard to hanging,
drawing, and quartering that I can find recorded evidence of
our executioners accepting bribes for what we might call "quick
dispatch." A case of one, John James, is dealt with in a tract. The
hangman demanded money of him "that he might be favourable
at his death," and brusquely put the sum at £20. James pleaded
poverty and could not rise to even £5: whereupon the hangman
said he "would torture him exceedingly." James said he must "leave
that to his mercy … however, the sheriff and hangmen were so civil
to him in his execution as to suffer him to be dead before he was
cut down." *It droppeth as the gentle rain from heaven*, Shakespeare
tells us of the quality of mercy. And there it was in full flush in
sheriff and hangman. That is as it should be.

As a matter of purely academic interest it may be stated that
only in the Year of Grace 1950 was drawing and quartering legally
abolished in Scotland, though it has long been out of fashion
even there. In the great days of hanging, drawing, and quartering,
London Bridge and Westminster Bridge were favourite places for
the exhibition of the carved-up corpse. It is interesting to trace the
history of the decline in punishment through the ages, beginning
with hanging, drawing, and quartering; to consider the Golden
Age, beginning in the reign of Henry VIII, in which there were
72,000 executions; then look at the last century, when in Britain
there were 220 offences for which one could be hanged. In those

happy and lively days, when England was rising to her greatness on the backs of inferior peoples, a man, woman, or child down to sixteen years of age, could be hanged for:

> Causing damage to Westminster Bridge
> Appearing disguised on a public road
> Cutting down young trees
> Shooting rabbits
> Stealing the value of five shillings (less than an American dollar)
> Stealing anything whatsoever from a bleach field
> Writing to extort money
> Returning prematurely from transportation
> Associating with Gypsies.

In the end hanging became so frivolous that it broke down because juries were refusing to convict—in spite of protests from the judges. Finally, from, say, 1850 to the present day, when we have come to the stage at which less than a dozen people are hanged every year. In contemporary Britain a boy becomes legally liable for military service and qualified by age for hanging when he reaches his eighteenth birthday, though until 1908 a child of sixteen could be hanged. In each age the supporters of the death penalty maintain that restrictions in its application would mean a subsequent increase in the particular crime for which it is applied. It must, in fairness, be said that history has steadily given them the lie, which in many parts of the world has been securely nailed to the table. Chief Justice Ellenborough, speaking in the Lords' debate of 1810 regarding a suggestion to repeal the law which made hanging the penalty for theft to the value of five shillings, said: "Repeal this law and see the contrast—no man can trust himself an hour out of doors without the most alarming apprehensions that, on his return, every vestige of his property will be swept off by the hardened robber." This statement appears to us ridiculous. It was. The last instance of hanging and drawing occurred at Derby in 1817. It was a case of high treason. By the special mercy of the Prince Regent the quartering of the three accused persons was remitted, and beheading substituted. The execution was public and the men hung for half an hour. On the platform, in front of the gallows, were placed the block and two sacks of sawdust; and on a bench two axes, two sharp knives, and a basket. Because of public fury the scaffold was surrounded by a great force of cavalry with drawn swords; several companies of infantry were also present. The space in front of the jail was densely packed with spectators. The poet Shelley is said to have been an eye-witness, which may account for his strong views and some of the things he has written.

Hanging, etc., Bulwarks of the Constitution

When Sir Samuel Romilly agitated against the continuance of hanging, drawing, and quartering—in the good old days castration preceded the disembowelling—the Law Officers of the Crown declared he was "breaking down the bulwarks of the Constitution." Glorious bulwarks. Now only hanging remains, and if that goes completely (it is already on the move) where will the Constitution be? We cannot have a Constitution without bulwarks—that is obvious, so the only thing we can do is to conserve the art of hanging by every means in our power.

England's Official Church Favours Hanging

If it were not that the prestige of the Church of England has so deplorably declined, I would suggest a strong appeal to the bishops on behalf of the hangman's rapidly disappearing art. Christian Churches can usually be relied upon to support State killing: in 1810 there were six bishops and an archbishop in the majority of thirty-two votes to eleven which defeated the measure to abolish hanging for the theft of five-shillings' worth of anything, and 5s., as you know, is now less than an American dollar. It must be a great comfort to all our hangmen to think that today they can be equally sure of Christian support for a continuance of their office.

Indeed, when we come to look squarely at the present position in regard to the death penalty in England it will be found that its two greatest supporters are the Law and the Church, as they always have been in the past; for which, may the Lord make us truly thankful. Readers know that one of the favourite political arguments in favour of the death penalty is that *public opinion demands it*. If I am not mistaken, Pontius Pilate, a staunch representative of Law and Order, used a similar argument in relation to a famous political execution about which he had to give the final decision. Home Secretaries may have forgotten the case, but if a *New Testament* should ever come their way, they can read it in the Gospels: time permitting. It is a well-written, moving story.

ENGLAND'S PUBLIC HANGINGS

From the last public ceremony of hanging and drawing at Derby in 1817 to the last public hanging in Britain in 1868 was a period of decline and deterioration in hanging. So-called advances in the law reduced the number of capital offences, and with one or two exceptions English hangmen of the period were below standard. The one good aspect of it was that hangings took place in public for all to see. Many of those public hangings provided an excuse for a public holiday, a kind of festival or English *fiesta* for which people dressed up, took a day off, got tight, and thoroughly enjoyed themselves. What nostalgia this inspires! That period in the nineteenth century was reminiscent of the glorious years of the great Queen Elizabeth's reign in Merrie England, when the whole population of London would turn out, the criminals to be executed would be exhibited in carts drawn through the main thoroughfares, and the good hangman Jack Ketch accompany them for all to see. Those were the days! But in the nineteenth century a powerful spirit of hypocrisy seized the English ruling class which thought that, because certain scenes at public hangings were unseemly, therefore public hangings must be abolished. Besides, those who said that capital punishment was a deterrent to crime were having a great laugh turned against them: everybody knew that there was more thieving and pocket-picking during a public hanging than at any other period—and this at a time when a man could be hanged for such crimes! It was something, to quote words once used jocularly by Winston S. Churchill, "up with which one could not put." And so public hanging was stopped. Then began the steady movement which has made it in England a hole-and-corner job conducted in great secrecy and now referred to by its shaken supporters as if it were something to be ashamed of, something better not discussed! In order to show what is being missed I cannot do better than give the best account I can find of the last public execution enjoyed by Londoners. I shall be doing a public service by putting it on record in this book.

The Bold Fenian Men of Oul' Ireland

It is not without significance that the last man to be publicly hanged in Britain—in front of London's old Newgate Prison, 26th May, 1868—was an Irish rebel, and a Fenian at that. He was Michael Barrett and his name is inscribed on the roll of honour of the Bold Fenian Men:

> We may have good men,
> But we'll never have better:
> Glory O—Glory O
> To the boul' Fenian Men!

—a song still popular in the Emerald Isle. Well, a number of those Bold Fenian Men attempted to rescue their comrades from Clerkenwell Prison by blowing in the jail wall with gunpowder. Seven people were killed when the barrel of powder exploded: a most unfortunate accident. Barrett produced witnesses to prove that he was in Glasgow when the accident occurred. The Crown—the State, that is—produced an informer named Patrick

Mullany, who turned "Queen's Evidence," or in other words he double-crossed his fellow countrymen, and gave evidence that Barrett was in London. Some very doubtful and highly suspect witnesses then came forward to identify Barrett, and although all others present at the event were quite unable to identify him, the English jurymen took the evidence of the informer and doubtfuls as good enough in the circumstances: the circumstances being that, on Michael Barrett's own showing, he was involved in the Fenian Movement. The Fenian Movement was inspired by the Irish Republican Brotherhood, a revolutionary body formed in New York in 1858 with the avowed aim of establishing an Irish Republic independent of Britain. That was enough for a patriotic English jury. In times of political stress or hysteria it is usually sufficient to prove that a man or woman has been *associated* with some person, body, association, party, or belief for a properly chosen jury to find him or her guilty of some perhaps major or capital crime. The method and technique is known to all attentive students of law and politics. The Irish regarded Michael Barrett as a patriot; to the English he was an abominable traitor. Some newspapers described his trial and condemnation to death as an act of justice. Others described his execution as judicial murder. We are not here concerned with anything but the public hanging of Barrett, for which a vast concourse of spectators assembled. *Reynolds's Newspaper* (31/3/1868) gave a full report of the ceremony, and I quote verbatim from it:

Account of England's Last Public Hanging

"His clergyman came first. Barrett mounted the steps with the most perfect firmness. This may seem a stereotyped phrase, but it really means more than is generally imagined. To ascend a ladder with one's arms and hands closely pinioned would at all times be difficult, but to climb a ladder to go to certain death might try the nerves of the boldest. Barrett walked up coolly and boldly. His face was as white as marble, but still he bore himself with firmness, and his demeanour was as far removed from bravado as from fear. We would not dwell on these details, but from the singular reception he met as he came out upon the scaffold. There was a burst of cheers, which was instantly accompanied by some few hisses, and so it remained for some seconds, till as the last moment approached the roars dwindled down to a dead silence. To neither cheers nor hisses did the culprit make the slightest recognition. He seemed only attentive to what the priest was saying to him, and to be engaged in fervent prayer. The hangman instantly put the cap over his face and the rope around his neck. Then Barrett, turning, spoke through his cap, and asked for the rope to be altered, which the hangman did. In another moment Barrett was a dead man. After the bolt was drawn, and the drop fell with a loud boom which always echoes from it, Barrett never moved. He died without a struggle. It is worthy of remark that a great cry rose from the crowd as the culprit fell—a cry which was neither an exclamation nor a scream, but partook in its sounds of both. With the fall of the drop the crowd began to disperse, but an immense mass waited till the time for cutting down came, and when nine o'clock struck there were calls of, 'Come on, body-snatcher!' 'Take away the man you've killed,' etc. The hangman appeared and cut down the body amid such a storm of yells and execrations as has seldom been heard even from such a crowd. There was nothing more then to be seen, so the concourse broke up."

The unseemly behaviour on the part of the public brought about the abandonment of public executions in Britain. This is a perfect example of the damage that can be done to a fine old institution by hen-brained people who did not realize that nothing could be more likely to bring hanging into hatred, ridicule, and contempt than such behaviour as that recorded above. As a result we have no more public hangings in Britain, which must be a great loss to the tourist traffic.

The most simple-minded person is always capable of moralizing on neck-breaking or any other question. But the least instructed English person knows that, as a people, the English have been singularly fortunate in more respects than one. Not least of these is that, in their good and reliable hangmen, they have, by lofty flights in political ethics, produced a class of formidable public servants. These hangmen are the Struldbrugs, the immortals, of a code of political morals which has stood the test of time for over one thousand years of our island's history. Governments come and go, but whatever their colour, from Prussian blue to watery pink, each one retains the Men of The Gallows, the respected Struldbrugs of the moral edifice upon which our existence depends. That the English feel uncomfortable when there is slackness in hanging was demonstrated in May 1959, when Mr. Silverman, a Labour Member of Her Majesty's Opposition, called for complete abolition of the death penalty in this realm. No less than fifty gallant Tory Members charged forward demanding its reinstatement for offences for which it had been stopped in 1957. This, after two years of partial abolition, during which the increase in all capital crimes amounted to 0.1 percent per month over the average rate for the last five years when the penalty of hanging was in full swing! It is no use arguing that the increase in murders of 0.1 percent a month over a short period proves nothing. It is *quite* enough to start off a campaign against abolition. Party politics are involved! So that, in Merrie England it can become a question of what government is in power whether a man hangs or lives: as it has already been in Queensland, Australia. A change in government may save life or kill: which is as it ought to be in any enlightened country. Such things as this are representative of the checks and balances which enable the English political system to roll on from precedent to precedent, broad based upon the people's will.

Hangmen Born, Not Made

Enough! On with the hanging! We may now consider in some detail the hangman's art, as practiced by one of the greatest exponents thereof who ever lived. I mean, of course, the late Mr. Berry, a bluff Yorkshireman, who was the very soul of honour and good nature. You already know that there are no published regulations in England governing the appointment of hangmen. Their assistants are appointed by the Prison Commissioners for particular executions and, like doctors and lawyers, they are paid by fees for work actually done. Chief hangmen are appointed by sheriffs from lists of assistants who have shown general aptitude and discretion; and chief hangmen are also paid by fee.

As there are usually some fifteen men qualified,[40] and now not a dozen hangings in the course of a twelvemonth, at fifteen guineas a drop the rewards for individuals are not great. Furthermore, the freedom of hangmen is greatly restricted by a host of pernickety restrictions which ought to be abolished. They may not write for the Press, or go on lecture tours in America. Mr. Berry tells us that in his youth he thought he had inborn ability which (if only cultivated by a little practice and reinforced by deep study) would make him a great artist. He says that when he applied for the post it was not from any special liking for it but because he was "simply driven to it by the poverty-stricken condition of his family." A curious factor that, one which has been rediscovered recently by our Industrial Health Research Board in regard to workers generally. In 1936 they announced (the Board, I mean) that "one of the most important factors in determining efficiency and pleasure in work is the inclination or will to work, and this, in turn, is largely dependent upon the provision of effective incentives." The Board goes on to state profoundly: "Of these incentives the most potent is probably the weekly wage," which shows that Mr. Berry was acting in accordance with deeply rooted psychological principles, common to men and women in other phases of life. It is as well to bear this clearly in mind, even if the rewards for hanging are not great. Testimonies to Mr. Berry's character show that he was a cool, businesslike, deeply religious man, and tender-hearted to a fault. The editor of his incomparable treatise[41] writes:

> When he has been due to start for a place of execution, his repugnance to the task has been so great that his wife and her mother have been obliged to use the greatest possible force of persuasion to prevent him from shirking his duty.

One can imagine the wife saying to herself: "If the jackass doesn't do the job, bang goes my Spring costume."

HANGMAN'S VERSES FOR HIS CLIENT

His hobbies were fishing, otter-hunting, shooting pigeons and rabbits; he adored animals. When Mr. Berry first applied for the post of executioner in 1883 there were 1,399 other applicants for the job. He was unlucky but, nothing daunted, he returned to his studies; and later applied again. This time he was successful. As he himself says, "There is a tide in the affairs of men, etc." From that day he never looked back. It is, of course, by way of apology he says that he was driven to the practice of hanging by the poverty-stricken condition of his family—mere bashfulness on his part. Obviously he was born for the work. When he went to measure a client for the gallows, he used (after having examined the neck) to hand the condemned man a piece of paper with these lines upon it:

> My brother—sit and think,
>> While yet on earth some hours are left to thee;
> Kneel to thy God, who does not from thee shrink,
>> And lay thy sins on Christ, who died for thee.
>
> He rests His wounded hand
>> With loving-kindness on thy sin-stained brow
> And says, "Here at thy side I ready stand
>> To make thy scarlet sins as white as snow.
>
> "I did not shed My blood
>> For sinless angels good and pure and true;
> For hopeless sinners flowed that crimson blood,
>> My heart's blood ran for you, My son, for you.
>
> "Though thou hast grieved Me sore,
>> My arms of mercy still are open wide,

I still hold open Heaven's shining door
  Come, then, take refuge in My wounded side.

"Men shun thee—but not I.
  Come close to Me, I love My erring sheep.
My blood can cleanse thy sins of blackest dye.
  I understand, if thou can'st only weep.

"Words fail thee—never mind.
  The Saviour can read e'en a sigh, a tear;
I came, sin-stricken hearts to heal and bind
  And died to save thee; to My heart thou'rt dear
"Come now: the time is short.
  Longing to pardon and to bless I wait.
Look up to Me, My sheep so dearly bought,
  And say, 'Forgive me ere it is too late.'"

Which shows that Mr. Berry believed in God the Father, God the Son, and possibly God the Holy Ghost also. It is true that his actual performances at hanging had not the same crispness of style as those of the late Mr. Calcraft nor, I should say, the limpid grace of our unparalleled Mr. Hangman Pierrepoint's work. Calcraft showed that, no matter how a hangman may reveal in his art the results of subconscious action, the final results are attained through lofty flights of the artist's own imagination; or else precisely as prophets receive religious truth.

The *Scienza Nuova*

Nevertheless, Mr. Berry's book is a diffusion of the ideals of a modest, laborious and useful life; it is to him that we owe many small, though important, improvements in the gallows. After him we may speak of the whole business of execution in this country as a *Scienza Nuova* of great delicacy, one to be practiced only by men of lyrical intuition and undoubted skill. Mr. Berry it was who laid the foundations for the mathematics of drops. His celebrated formula:[42]

$$\frac{412}{(\text{Weight of the body in stones})} \quad = \quad \left(\begin{array}{c}\text{length of drop} \\ \text{in feet}\end{array}\right)$$

is with slight modification used to this day. He it was who discovered that a three-quarter-inch rope of five strands of Italian hemp is the best for hanging men. Four strands will suffice for many women; and even three work well enough for infants.

Mr. Berry first used the brass eyelet; a marvellous technical advance.

A WICKED CALUMNY REFUTED

At this point I must beg the reader to pause with me for a moment while I refute a very wicked calumny against the well-established reputation of this notable hangman. I had heard something of it years ago in Dublin, but not until 7th December, 1947, did I ever see the wickedness in cold print; and you would never suspect who was the perpetrator thereof. It was no other than Mr. James Harpole, F.R.S., one of Britain's most distinguished living surgeons, who also writes well—a rare combination. In his reminiscences (which were serialized in the *Sunday Chronicle*) appeared a statement which I had to read several times to be sure that I was not still half asleep—one of the few luxuries we can enjoy in these times is to read the sabbath newspapers over a cup of tea in bed—when suddenly the enormity of Mr. Harpole's words struck me like the blast from an atomic bomb exploding nearby. They were to the following effect: that a well-known nineteenth-century figure about Trinity College, Dublin, a most benevolent septuagenarian, the Rev. Samuel Haughton, Doctor of Divinity, Doctor of Medicine, Doctor of Laws, Fellow of T.C.D., Fellow of the Royal Society, formerly a Professor of Geology and famous for the treatises he had written on Mathematics, had worked out the formula for the scientific long drop since then used by our hangmen. Mr. Harpole quotes *sheer hear-say evidence* for this allegation, for which, I am happy to note, he himself takes no responsibility whatever. A third-year medical student it was who imparted the information about Sammy Haughton, saying that the latter could not bear to think of murderers strung up and left to kick and dangle until they suffocated. Hence, the kindly reverend gentleman used his rare combination of qualifications to work out the scientific formula by which any hangman could calculate, after weighing his client, what distance in space the body should be allowed to fall in order not merely to fracture the neck but kill instanter. Mr. Harpole significantly comments: "I gazed at the old man fascinated. He looked so gentle. It seemed incongruous." Now, the whole point is that in his wonderful book Mr. Berry has established for all time the truth of the matter: that it was his predecessor in office Mr. Hangman Marwood (A.D. 1874–88) who invented the long drop and that it was he, Mr. Berry, who evolved the scientific formula used by his successors in our progressive country ever since. Thus Mr. Berry occupies a place in the science of hanging as important as that of Albert Einstein in general scientific thought, and Mr. Berry's *Theory of Hanging* must be regarded as in a category hardly less nebulous than Einstein's *Theory of Relativity*. It was Mr. Berry who found the constant. Mr. Berry found that mystical number 412 in the formula, and his mastery of hangmanship was recognized by rulers and public long before Haughton became a gownsman in Trinity College, Dublin. I make no apology for introducing this refutation of what can only be regarded as a most wicked calumny, one started by the Lord only knows whom, disseminated by that third-year gasbag medical student and in all honesty but disconcertingly brought up again by Mr. James Harpole, F.R.S. Let honour be given where it is due: to the author of that unique book of reminiscences, *My Experiences as an Executioner*, that perfectionist in the scientific side of the art of hanging. Having thus cleared Mr. Hangman Berry's name, we may well proceed. Before doing so, however, I think I ought to quote the very latest and most authoritative statement I know about the drop. Under the heading "Judicial

Hanging" the *British Medical Journal* (16/7/1947) published the following dialogue on officially caused death:

> Q. *What is the length of the drop in a judicial hanging?*
> A. On an average six feet (1.8 metres), varying inversely with the weight of the body. The knot is placed at the angle of the jaw, and the object is to jerk the head sideways, fracture or dislocate the vertebral column, and rupture the spinal cord. This happens *almost invariably*, the dislocation usually occurring between the second and third cervical vertebrae. Although some other structures may be damaged, the strain is not nearly enough to divide the muscles and ligaments completely.

I have italicized the words "almost invariably" for they must mean that the medical scientist who wrote the above is not convinced that it always happens. Nor indeed is anybody. Not that this matters greatly, because the operative word in the judge's sentence—"to be hanged by the neck until he is dead"—is *until*. "Until he is dead" covers everything, including those little misfortunes of hangmen when they do a botched job on those occasions when, like the rest of us, they get out of the wrong side of the bed.

SPILSBURY ON THE DROP

The great Sir Bernard Spilsbury, M.D., who for many years was the principal scientific witness—pathologist—for the prosecution in murder trials in England, was deeply interested in judicial hanging. In his long experience of post-mortem examinations of the hanged, he came to realize that the cervical spine of a human being could be broken at a more or less constant level. This was ably demonstrated again and again by the technical skill of modern hangmen. It set the great man thinking. Could this scientific fact be used for the advantage of the art and to help the hangman's clients?

Sir Bernard was at heart a humane man, and after due consideration of the problems involved—profound some of them, and involving ballistics and mathematics—he at last reached the conclusion that an *increase of three inches in the drop* would be an advance for the cause of humanitarianism. Such was his prestige that his recommendation was officially accepted—and this notwithstanding the deep conservatism which we find in almost everything relating to hangmanship. It is by such small advances as this that science progresses. We had most of us thought of English hanging as already perfect before the Spilsbury Amendment to the traditionally established drops (which had been reached by a long process of trial and error, and had stood the tests of time). One may well doubt whether any further advance is possible. Spilsbury was regarded as a perfectionist in everything he touched. He found forensic medicine to be highly suspect when he first entered the field. By his work, and his great forensic ability, he won the confidence of judges, juries, police, and prosecuting counsel; and in time even the hangmen of England, who at first regarded his interest in their art as the work of a meddlesome busybody, acknowledged his great virtues.

Another medical expert contributed some thoughtful remarks on hanging to the *British Medical Journal* of 10/12/1949. I quote: "The ideal, I was informed as part of my medical education many years ago, is for the odontoid peg to break the odontoid ligament and drive into the medulla, destroying the vital centres ... One would agree that the present method or *any conceivable method* of hanging does not cause instantaneous death, *because the adjective is inapplicable to any mode of death known to man*; but it approaches instantaneousness much more closely than any other method, even shooting, unless in that method a bullet actually traverses the medulla."

Hand-in-Hand with Science

Pointedly apropos is the hanging of Herbert Mills, aged nineteen, at Lincoln in December 1951, when the medical expert witness at the coroner's inquest declared that the hanged man's heart continued to beat for twenty minutes after the execution; that the man was dead "from all points of view"; and that the continued beating of the heart was a purely automatic function which did not in any sense indicate that life continued. In view of the wonderful advances in medical knowledge, the mere layman has a right to ask this question: Would it have been possible, if every measure known to science had been applied, to revive this hanged man? I have been assured by several medical friends that it would not have been difficult to revive him, and that, furthermore, the damage, if any, to the vertebrae could probably have been repaired. It would appear that a very wonderful opportunity may have been lost, for, by reviving and treating a man whose heart continued to beat, all controversy regarding the painlessness or painfulness of hanging might have been settled for all time. I trust official reassurances based upon such a resuscitation will one day be forthcoming, and thus demonstrate once more that hangmanship and medical science can march hand-in-hand when this is in the public interest.

Thus, as any good hangman will tell you, a good hanging kills quicker than a shooting. To sum up, the closer we examine it, the better hanging proves to be.

HANGING, FLOGGING, WAR AND SADISM

The American Chessman case (referred to elsewhere in this tour of crimes and punishments) rather shook the complacency of the English, who were proud of the record they had long held for the ferocity of their criminal law and the objective insensibility of their penal system. The cat o'-nine-tails (the famous ninelashed rope whip for flogging civilian criminals) was retained long after the flogging of lower-deck sailors had been abolished in the British Navy. But recent legislation curbed the activities of floggers and whippers and birchers in this England, and now, as with hanging, this sort of punishment has to fight for its very existence. However, the hangers and floggers never lose hope, and the year 1961 in which these lines are written is notable for (a) a revival of pro-hanging propaganda and (b) a similar revival in favour of an extension of the now limited scope for the cat and the birch. There was a heartening incident in 1960 at the time of the summer solstice when the sun appeared to be standing still above us, pausing before returning on his course. In reply to a question about flogging, a baker's dozen of Britain's managers of "approved schools" for young delinquents were wholeheartedly in favour of the cat-o'-nine tails for youths of 18 years of age. Furthermore, two of these chosen experts in juvenile education demanded the cat for boys of 16; and one imaginative manager recommended it for children of 10 years of age. Note that these official educators represent only one district of England—in the north-west. If they are at all representative of the others, one may say that there is a fairly solid body of what the government considers the most enlightened of our educators in favour of a return to the good old days of proper lambasting as an aid to progress. Their opinions confirmed a national poll on the subject, taken not many months earlier. It is argued by psychologists that the cry for bigger and better punishment of delinquents springs from either a natural sadism, or fear, or from the desire to foist on scape-goats the guilt rising from one thing or another: temperament, inefficiency, some form of inadequacy, or just helplessness. The same poll showed that British public opinion favours an increase in hangings. One should note the lack of psychological comfort in the failure of the 1960 Paris Summit Conference and consequently the apparent hopelessness of achieving anything useful in the way of disarmament, the publicized existence of vast stockpiles of frightful weapons—nuclear, chemical, bacteriological, and what have you—controlled by men in a genocidal profession frankly devoted to the potential elimination from this globe of man, beast, and civilization. We must never forget that the professional military man's training makes a natural or inclined killer into a professional killer; and that, in the last resort, it will be either a military or a political mind—and which is more dangerous is anybody's guess—that will decide upon the release of these horrific weapons. In this century there have already been two World Wars, each one appalling in its results for mankind. Both were started by a collaboration of politicians and finished by the military. Now they are all again collaborating as they were before, all ostensibly for defence purposes! In these circumstances there is no need to look far for very great reasons for fear, and fear is the basis of all kinds of neuroses. In sadism the neurotic and psychotic find releases, as the infamous Marquis de Sade made clear enough a long time ago. There can be a great release in hanging.

Having made this clear, we may return to our muttons.

THE LATE MR. BERRY ON HANGING

I have no doubt that, had Mr. High Hangman Berry's life been spared for a few years longer, he would have done for the gallows what the ingenious Germans did for the cycle: make it capable of climbing trees or conversion into a paddle-boat. The only thing necessary to turn this world into a perfect place for Mr. Berry was a permanent jury for all murder trials in England, that jury to consist of retired hangmen, rope-makers, hemp merchants, prison governors, eyelet makers, select members of police and prison services, not to mention members of the Upper Chamber, the Lords Spiritual and Temporal. And this in spite of the fact that Mr. Berry was not one of those men who are vindictive to five places of decimals, although he did not believe in close seasons for hanging. With these introductory remarks regarding the place of Mr. Berry in the general history of hanging we may now consider the words of wisdom that flowed from his honest pen:

VITAL IMPORTANCE OF THE DROP

"My method," says Mr. Berry in his magnum opus, "My method of execution is the outcome of the experience of my predecessors and myself, aided by suggestions from the doctors, and is rather the result of gradual growth than the invention of any one man. The matter which requires the greatest attention in connection with an execution is the allowance of a suitable drop for each person executed, and the adjustment of this matter is not *nearly* so simple as an outsider would imagine. It is, of course, necessary that the drop should be of sufficient length to cause instantaneous death, that is to say, to cause death by dislocation rather than by strangulation and on the other hand, the drop must not be so great as to *outwardly* mutilate the victim. If all murderers who have to be hanged were of precisely the same weight and build it would be very easy to find out the most suitable length of drop, and always to give the same; but as a matter of fact they differ enormously. In the earliest days of hanging it was the practice for the executioner to place his noose round the victim's neck, and then to haul upon the other end of the rope (which was passed through a ring on the scaffold-pole) until the culprit was strangled without any drop at all. After a while the drop system was introduced, but the length of drop given was never more than three feet, so that death was still generally caused by strangulation and not by dislocation, as it is at present.

Mr. Marwood—Pioneer of the New Science

"One after another, all our English executioners followed the same plan without thought of change or improvement, until Mr. Marwood took the appointment. He, as a humane man, carefully considered the subject, and came to the conclusion that the then existing method, though certain, was not so rapid or painless as it ought to be. In consequence he introduced his long-drop system with a fall of from seven to ten feet, which causes instantaneous death by severance of the spinal cord. I was slightly acquainted with Mr. Marwood before his death, and I had gained some particulars of his method from conversation with him; so that when I undertook my first execution, at Edinburgh, I naturally worked upon his lines. This first commission was to execute Robert

Vickers and William Innes, two miners, who were condemned to death for the murder of two gamekeepers. The respective weights were 10 stone 4 lb. and 9 stone 6 lb., and I gave them drops of 8 ft. 6 in. and 10 ft. respectively. In both cases death was instantaneous, and the prison surgeon gave me a testimonial to the effect that the execution was satisfactory in every respect.

A Rough Working List of Drops

"Upon this experience I based a table of weights and drops. Taking a man of 14 stone as basis, and giving him a drop of 8 ft., which is what is thought necessary, I calculated that every half-stone lighter weight would require a two inches longer drop, and the full table as I entered it in my time, stood as follows:

14	stone	8 ft.	10 in.
13½	"	8 "	2 "
13	"	8 "	4 "
12½	"	8 "	6 "
12	"	8 "	8 "
11½	"	8 "	10 "
11	"	9 "	0 "
10½	"	9 "	2 "
10	"	9 "	4 "
9½	"	9 "	6 "
9	"	9 "	8 "
8½	"	9 "	10 "
8	"	10 "	0 "

"This table[44] I calculated for persons of what I might call 'average' build, but it could not by any means be rigidly adhered to with safety. For instance, I have more than once had to execute persons who had attempted suicide by cutting their throats, or who had been otherwise wounded about the neck, and to prevent reopening the wounds I have reduced the drop by nearly half.

DOCTORS' ADVICE ON HANGING

"Again, in the case of persons of very fleshy build, who often have weak bones and muscles about the neck, I have reduced the drop by a quarter or half the distance indicated by the table. If I had not done so, no doubt two or three of those whom I have executed would have had their heads entirely jerked off[45]—which did occur in one case to which I shall again refer. In the case of persons with scrofulous tendencies, it is especially necessary that the fall should be unusually short, and in these cases I have at times received useful hints from the jail doctors.

THE GOODALE MESS EXPLAINED

"Until November 30, 1885, I worked to the scale already given, but on that date I had the awful experience above referred to, which caused me to reconsider the whole subject and to construct a general table on what I believe to be a truly scientific basis ... The man with whom it occurred was Robert Goodale, whom I executed at Norwich Castle. He weighed 15 stone, and the drop indicated by the first table would therefore be 7 ft. 8 in., but in consequence of his appearance I reduced it to 5 ft. 9 in., because the muscles of his neck did not appear well developed and strong. But even this, as it turned out, was not short enough, and the result was *one* of the most horrible mishaps that I have ever had. As will be seen from the full report of this case ... the coroner exonerated me from all blame, and testified to the careful way in which I had done my work; but I felt that it was most necessary to take every possible precaution against the recurrence of such an affair. I therefore worked out a table of the striking force of falling bodies of various weights falling through different distances.[46] Working with this I calculate that an 'average' man, of any weight, requires a fall that will finish with a striking force of 24 cwt., and if the convict seems to require less, I *mentally* estimate the striking force that is necessary, and then by referring to the table I can instantly find the length of drop required. To see how this new table works out we may take the case of Robert Goodale again. As he weighed 15 stone his striking force with a drop of 2 ft. would be 21 cwt. 21 lb., or with a drop of 3 ft., 26 cwt. 7 lb., so that if he were a man of ordinary build the drop necessary would be 2 ft. 6 in. As I estimated from his appearance that his drop ought to have been about one-sixth less than the standard, I should have given him, working on this new table, about 2 ft. 1 in. instead of the 5 ft. 9 in. which was actually given. This is an extreme case, with a very heavy man, but all through the table it will be found that the drop works out shorter than in the first table. For instance, Vickers and Innes, the two Edinburgh murderers previously referred to, would have had their drops reduced from 8 ft. 6 in. and 10 ft. to 5 ft. 6 in. and 7 ft. respectively, if they had been treated according to the present revised table.

Doctor who Erred

"On August 20, 1881, at Kirkdale Jail, Liverpool, at the execution of John Conway, an attempt was made to dictate to me the length of drop, and a most unfortunate scene ensued. From seeing the convict, Conway, I had decided that the drop ought to be 4 ft. 6 in., a little under the scale rate, and I was surprised and annoyed at being told by Dr. Barr, acting, I believe, under authority, that I was to give a drop of 6 ft. 9 in. I said that it would pull the man's head off altogether, and finally refused to go on with the execution if such a long drop were given. Dr. Barr then measured off a shorter drop, some ten or twelve inches shorter, but still much longer than I thought necessary, and I reluctantly agreed to go on. The result, everyone knows. The drop was not so long as to absolutely pull off the victim's head, but it ruptured the principal blood vessels of the neck.

"I do not know who[49] was really responsible for the interference with my calculation, but do not think that the long drop was Dr. Barr's own idea, as the drop which I suggested was on the same system as he had previously commended, and was almost identical with the drop that would have worked out on the basis of his own recommendation in a letter to *The Times* some years ago.

A HANGMAN'S DIPLOMA

"Dr. Barr's letter to me, written in 1884, was as follows:

> 1, St. Domingo Grove,
> Everton, Liverpool,
> Sept. 2nd, 1884.

Sir,

In compliance with your request, I have pleasure in giving you a certificate as to the manner in which you conducted the execution of Peter Cassidy in H.M. Prison, Kirkdale. I may now repeat the statement which I gave in evidence at the Inquest, 'that I have never seen an execution more satisfactorily performed.' This was very gratifying to me.

Your rope was of excellent quality; fine, soft, pliable, and strong. You adjusted the ring directed forwards in the manner in which I have recommended in my pamphlet, *Judicial Hanging*. You gave a sufficient length of drop, considering the weight of the culprit, and completely dislocated the atlas and axis (first and second vertebrae). I have reckoned that the weight of the criminal multiplied by the length of the drop, might range from 1,120 to 1,260 foot-pounds, and I have calculated that this *vis viva* in the case of Cassidy amounted to 1,140 foot pounds.

The pinioning and other details were carried out with due decorum. I hope, whoever be appointed to the post of Public Executioner may be prohibited from also performing the part of a 'showman' to gratify a depraved and morbid public curiosity.[50]

> James Barr, M.D.,
> Medical Officer, H.M. Prison,
> Kirkdale.

To Mr. James Berry.

"The rope I use is thirteen feet long and has a one-inch brass ring worked into one end, through which the other end of the rope is passed to form the noose. A leather washer, which fits the rope pretty tightly, is used to slip up behind the brass ring, in order to prevent the noose slipping or slackening after it has been adjusted.

"In using the rope I always adjust it with the ring just behind the left ear. This position I never alter, though, of course, if there were any special reason for doing so, for instance, if the convict had attempted suicide and were wounded on the side of the throat, death could be caused by placing the ring under the chin or even behind the head.

How Hanging Kills

"The position behind the ear, however, has distinct advantages and is the best calculated to cause instantaneous and painless death, because it acts in three different ways towards the same end. In the first place, it will cause death by strangulation, which was really the only cause of death in the old method of hanging, before the long drop was introduced. Secondly, it dislocates the vertebrae, which is now the actual cause of death. And thirdly, if a third factor were necessary, it has a tendency to internally rupture the jugular vein, which in itself is sufficient to cause practically instantaneous death.

Note on Pinioning

"The pinioning arrangement, like the rest of the arrangements for an execution, is very simple. A broad leather body-belt is clasped round the convict's waist, and to this the arm-straps are fastened. Two straps, an inch and a half wide, with strong steel buckles, clasp the elbows and fasten them to the body-belt, while another strap of the same strength goes round the wrists, and is fastened into the body-belt in front. The legs are pinioned by means of a single two-inch strap below the knees. The rest of the apparatus consists of a white[51] cap, shaped somewhat like a bag, which pulls down over the eyes of the criminal to prevent his seeing the final preparations.

NOTE ON SCAFFOLDS

"Until recently the scaffolds in use in the various jails differed very much in the details of their construction, as there was no official model, but in each case the local authorities followed their own idea. In 1885, however, a design was drawn, in the Surveyor's Department of the Home Office, by Lieut.-Col. Alten Beamish, R.E. Before being finally adopted, the design was submitted to me; and it seemed a thoroughly good one, as, indeed, it has since proved to be, in actual practice. The design is supplied to the authorities of any jail where a scaffold is to be erected, from the Engineer's Department at the Home Office; and, with a slight alteration, has been the pattern in general use to the present day. The alteration of which I speak is a little one suggested by myself, and consists of the substitution of a slope, or a level gangway, in place of steps. I have found, in some cases, when the criminals were nervous or prostrated, that the steps formed a practical difficulty. The slope, or gangway, was approved by the Home Office, and was first used on April 15, 1890, at Kirkdale Jail, for the execution of Wm. Chadwick. It was a simple improvement, but it has turned out to be a very useful one." (Mr. Berry's inborn modesty will be observed throughout this description of his official duties. Incidentally, it was only in 1937 that modern science was able to improve on his machinery.) "At most of the jails in the country the scaffold is taken to pieces and laid away immediately after use, but in Newgate, Wandsworth, Liverpool, and Strangeways (Manchester), it is kept standing permanently. The essential parts of the scaffold are few. There is a heavy crossbeam, into which bolts terminating in hooks are usually fastened. In some cases this crossbeam stands on two upright posts, but usually its ends are let into the walls of the scaffold-house. Of course, the hooks fastened to it are intended to hold the rope. The scaffold proper, or trap, or drop, as it is variously called, is the portion of the structure to which most importance is attached, and of which the Government furnishes a plan. It consists of two massive oaken doors, fixed in an oak framework on a level with the floor, and over a deep, bricked pit. The arrangement is a very good one as both doors must necessarily fall at exactly the same moment." (At a recent execution, a hangman's engineer fell into the pit with the client. At another, the drop worked but did not kill the client, who remarked: "What do you take me for? A b——— Yo-Yo!") "Their great weight—for they are of three-inch oak—causes them to drop very suddenly, even without the weight of the criminal, and they are caught by spring catches to prevent any possibility of rebound.

Hangman Describes Hanging

"The hour fixed for execution is 8:00 am.,[52] in all the prisons, except Wandsworth and Lincoln, where it is 9:00 a.m. Of course, the scaffold and rope are arranged, and the drop decided, beforehand. I calculate for three minutes to be occupied from the time of entering the condemned cell to the finish of life's great tragedy for the doomed man, so I enter the cell punctually at three minutes to eight. In order that my action in hanging a man may be legal, it is necessary that I should have what is known as an 'Authority to Hang,' which is drawn up and signed by the Sheriff, and handed to me a few minutes before the time of the execution.

An "Order to Hang"

Its form varies a good deal. In some cases it is a long, wordy document, full of the 'wherefores' and 'whatsoevers' in which the law delights. But usually it is a simple, official-looking form, engrossed by the jail clerk, and running somewhat as follows:

To JAMES BERRY

I ...., of ...., in the County of ...., Esquire, Sheriff of the said County of ...., do hereby authorize you to hang A............ B............ who now lies under Sentence of Death in Her Majesty's Prison at ....

Dated this .... day of ....
.... Sheriff.

"This is folded in three,[53] *and endorsed outside,*

Re A............... B...............
AUTHORITY TO HANG
.... Sheriff
.... shire

THE HOLY PROCESSION

"When we enter the condemned cell, the chaplain is already there, and has been for some time. Two attendants, who have watched through the convict's last night on earth, are also present. At my appearance the convict takes leave of his attendants, to whom he generally gives some little token or keepsake, and I at once proceed to pinion his arms. As soon as the pinioning is done, a procession is formed, and it used to be in the following order:

Chief Warder

Warder   Warder

CHAPLAIN

Warder   CONVICT   Warder

EXECUTIONER

Principal Warder   Principal Warder

Warder   Warder

Governor and Sheriff

Wand Bearer   Wand Bearer

Jail Surgeon and Attendant

Mr. Berry continues: "In some few cases, where the prisoner has not confessed before the time for the execution, I have approached him in the cell in a kindly manner, asking him, as it can make no difference to his fate, to confess the justice of the sentence, in order that I may feel sure that I am not hanging an innocent person." (Note Mr. Berry's precaution on behalf of his conscience.) "In most cases they have done so, either in the cell, or at the last moment on the scaffold. Of course the confidences reposed in me at such moments I have never divulged, and it would be most improper to do so; but I am at liberty to state that of all the people I have executed, only two or three have died without fully and freely confessing their guilt.

Last Scene of All

"On the way from the cell to the scaffold the chaplain reads the service for the burial of the dead, and as the procession moves I place the white cap upon the head of the convict. Just as we reach the scaffold I pull the cap over his eyes. Then I place the convict under the beam, pinion the legs just below the knees, with a strap similar to the one used for the elbows, adjust the rope, pull the bolt and the trap falls. Death is instantaneous, but the body is left hanging for at least half an hour *in case of accidents* [see page 138], and is then lowered into a coffin, made in the prison, and carried to the mortuary to await the inquest. The inquest usually takes place at ten o'clock, but in some few places it is held at noon. After the inquest the body is buried in the prison grounds." There is now no quick-lime used, and only the prison authorities know the exact place of burial. Flowers not permitted.

As Mr. Berry remarks, "In carrying out the last penalty of the law, *everything* is conducted with decorum and solemnity." It is comforting to have this assurance from a disinterested party, and if hangmen *do* sometimes make mistakes, we must not be hard on them.

They are not always to blame.

THOSE LAST FLEETING HOURS

For many years there have been few changes in what happens in our prisons, and what is quoted above may be taken as including the traditional fundamentals, except that nowadays a hanging is more perfunctory and accompanied by less solemnity and pageantry than in better and more spacious days. The Holy Procession is not always formed, and if there is a procession it is the procession of a drab age. I am deeply indebted to the *News of the World* (11/3/45), which, with our legal publications, is a most reliable guide to criminal happenings. Here is what is justifiably claimed by that excellent newspaper to be "an authentic description of the last fleeting hours" of a man waiting to be hanged: "At ten o'clock on the night before the execution two of six prison officers who have shared the death-watch shake their prisoner by the hand and wish him good-bye. Two others will have done the same thing eight hours earlier. The remaining couple take over from 10 p.m. until 7 a.m. next day. From the latter hour two officers who had not previously 'sat' with the condemned man keep the remaining two hours of the watch and accompany their prisoner to the execution shed. He will probably have spent most of his last night writing letters or playing cards with his guards. Few condemned men sleep at the end, though invariably they are quite calm and self-possessed when the realization comes that there is no more hope. At 7 a.m. the clothing in which the man has been tried and condemned is given to him minus collar and tie, and the prison attire destroyed. This, however, was not the procedure in the case of Karl Hulten, who, so it has been disclosed, went to the scaffold wearing prison clothes, doubtless to preserve his American uniform from ignominy. For breakfast, porridge, bacon, bread and butter are served to men who are to die within the hour. Some eat, some decline. The majority are content with a cup of tea and unlimited cigarettes. Between 8:30 and 9 o'clock the chaplain enters the condemned cell to give spiritual consolation. If he wishes the prisoner may take Holy Communion. The chaplain usually stays in the death cell until nine o'clock. At that moment the following will be standing quietly outside the door: The governor of the prison, the under-sheriff of the county, the executioner, assistant executioner, medical officer of the prison, chief officer of the prison, hospital orderly, and prison engineer.

Hangman Shakes Hands and Gets Busy

"On the stroke of nine, the cell door opens and the governor says to the under-sheriff, 'Your prisoner, sir.' Condemned persons are the prisoners of the High Sheriff of the county. At the same time the executioner steps in front of the condemned man and offers to shake hands with him. The gesture is invariably acknowledged. The hospital orderly proffers a tot of brandy, and the executioner's assistant pinions the condemned man's arms behind him above the elbow. All this takes a matter of seconds. The two officers of the death-watch then lead the condemned out of the cell to the execution shed, usually but a few steps away. Here he is guided to a chalk-mark on the trap. The executioner then pulls a white cap over the head and face of the prisoner, adjusts the noose of the rope already suspended just above by a single thread. At the same time the assistant executioner straps the prisoner's ankles. The executioner gives a sign for everyone to step off the trap, and quickly kicks the release bolt from the lever. It is all over."

Fabulous Speed of English Hangings

If there is one thing which those responsible for English hangings would wish the whole world to know, it is the fabulous speed of the final operation. Less than *twenty seconds* elapse from the moment the public executioner enters the condemned cell, until the hanged person is *dead*! That is the official pronouncement on the subject, as included in the evidence submitted to the 1953 Royal Commission under the chairmanship of Sir Ernest Gowers, a most distinguished and trusted man in Britain's public service. The evidence submitted showed such unanimous approbation of the efficiency of hanging, as the *quickest and most painless* method of dispatch from this world, that Sir Ernest Gowers curiously commented: "There is an association for euthanasia ... I can hardly believe that, if they are actually successful, they will choose the method of hanging." This remark of so level-headed a chairman savours somewhat of scepticism, as if he felt that the official evidence had been, shall we say, not "over-cooked" but "overdone." Perhaps it was. But, if it was, one must forgive officialdom on the grounds that, in a grave matter of this sort, one can hardly be too emphatic. As every reader of this book will have learnt by now, *English hanging cannot be beaten* when it is a matter of expedition and extreme virtuosity. The Report[54] of the 1953 Royal Commission proudly and rightly recorded that it did not believe that hanging "now admits of improvement"; that from cell to drop averages 17 seconds in England and 47½ seconds in Scotland; and that "*no mishap has taken place in the last 50 years*"! Is not such a record good enough for anybody?

SCAFFOLD UNAFFECTED BY PROGRESS, REVOLUTIONS, OR SELECT COMMITTEES

As we look round this world today, this rather sad world of wars, revolutions, unrest, and political puzzles, we find that there is at least one admirable tradition in the history of man which always survives the worst upheavals: the scaffold, or its equivalent. Leaders of revolutions, dictators, statesmen, and political philosophers—whatever their creed or colour—are all agreed on at least one point, and it is that, if society is to be reformed, pruned, polished, and improved, the reforms, prunings, polishings, and improvements cannot *possibly* be achieved without the aid of that oldest of institutions, the death penalty. It is true that there are countries and moments in which the legal erasure of human life is temporarily abolished, but sooner or later a Leader of Enlightenment appears who reverts to the good old tradition. Take Italy, for example. Capital punishment was abolished there in 1889, with the remarkable result that the homicide rate decreased steadily each year: from 10.64 per 100,000 of the population per annum to 3.48. But in our own times a great ruler appeared there who, in 1928, reintroduced the death penalty for attempts on his own life or even that of the king; and also for any crime "endangering the safety of the State." Thus, at one brilliant stroke, enlightenment came into its own again, thanks to the great Mussolini. In Germany the death penalty was almost entirely in abeyance until a statesman-prophet came into power in the nineteen-thirties. Then the supreme penalty was not only restored to its proper place in public affairs, but it was extended, thanks to the great Hitler. In Austria also capital punishment was abolished in 1919, to be reintroduced in 1934 by the government of the late Doctor Dollfuss, a little Catholic Gentleman.

And so it seems, from the experience of our very own times, that the scaffold is *one of the few political edifices which cannot be permanently swept away by the most enlightened revolution.* Indeed, it has always been more or less the same—everywhere, as a little research indicates.

The hangmen can feel secure in their jobs.

BRITAIN STANDS BY HER HANGMEN

If any reassurance is required on this point, one has only to read the Official Reports of the various Committees and Royal Commissions on Capital Punishment held in 1819, 1864, 1930, and 1949–50. The Select Committee which published its Report in December 1930 recommended the abolition of the death penalty for an experimental period of five years. The British Parliament did not act on that recommendation. Hangings continued. As we have seen, the House of Commons in April 1948 voted in favour of abolition and for a brief moment hanging was suspended—until the House of Lords *refused to confirm abolition*. The hangmen again got to work. Experience had now taught the State that it was unsafe to give a Royal Commission terms of reference which would enable it to submit a recommendation for the *abolition* of capital punishment. And so the latest Commission's chief claim to fame is that it collected and collated much useful information not otherwise easily available to the public. For example, a Home Office Memorandum submitted to the Commission, and strongly favouring retention of hanging, said that nowadays a man waiting to be hanged is allowed a daily pint of beer or stout on request; and ten cigarettes or half an ounce of tobacco. Unless, that is, there are medical reasons to the contrary. He is even permitted to smoke in his cell, we are assured by this benevolent department of State. One cannot but be thankful for all this weighty information, but one must not be surprised or disappointed if nothing is ever officially whispered about strangulations, slow deaths, botched hangings, and innocent men hanged.

The Last Certificate

The hangmen are there for public service. What they do is perfect. The less the public knows about the final reality the better it is for all. From the point of view of the Government the only formalities required after a criminal is hanged in England are (a) the posting outside the prison of a certificate of death signed by an official surgeon and (b) that quick inquest at which no answers are ever given to any but the few questions which the State permits to be answered. As this book is nearing its end I cannot do better than reproduce exactly the wording of this important certificate:

> I .... the Surgeon of His/Her Majesty's Prison of
> .... hereby certify that I this day examined the
> Body of .... on whom Judgement of Death was
> this day executed in the said Prison; and that on that
> Examination I found that the said .... was
> dead.
>
> Dated this .... day of ....

You will notice that the word "surgeon" is used to describe the Medical Officer who signs this certificate. Judicial hanging in Britain, it would seem, is officially regarded as a surgical operation. Hence, the certificate of a surgeon is no doubt more appropriate than that of a physician. And there are other reasons which spring to the mind.

But enough has surely been said to show that, in Old England at least, hanging is well done from beginning to end. Let us forget the heads occasionally pulled off by bad hangmen, and the strangulation which may happen—through no *fault* of the hangman. All we need remember are those impressive words uttered by the august judges: "To be hanged by the neck *until dead*." UNTIL DEAD—those are the operative words.

In executing the Judgment of Death, the hangman never fails. And nothing else matters to the State.

THE NEW HOMICIDE ACT OF 1957

In the years 1955–56 there was a vigorous campaign against capital punishment in Britain, and very well organized it proved to be. It was a signal for several distinguished authors to write books on the subject, and, one may say that all of them were against a practice which they regarded as out-moded and ineffective; some went so far as to say it was "utterly barbarous." Mr. Sidney Silverman, a Labour Member of Parliament, in 1956 introduced a simple little Bill for complete abolition of this time-honoured institution. The Bill was passed by a majority in the House of Commons on a *free vote* of the House, and those who had the best interests of hangmen at heart began to tremble for their cause. These, to repeat once more, represent a nucleus of the most distinguished people in this old country: Lords Spiritual and Temporal, Law Lords and Judges of the High Court, the vast majority of titled people from Dukes to Baronets, many great landowners and business tycoons; and all of them ornaments of contemporary society and Members of that Unwritten Establishment of this country whose will rules the populace. This undefined but ever-present English Establishment resembles the unwritten English Constitution which, by its duration, all-embracing powers, flexibility, and sheer utility in practice, is the admiration of the civilized world. As that wise French author La Fontaine put it:

> The reasoning of the stronger is always the best.

And so it was that the Silverman Bill got short shrift when it went to the House of Lords, where all the good, reliable peers lived well up to tradition and, by virtue of their strong reasoning, tore it to shreds. The Bill for total abolition aroused their sense of shame: and shame is virtue's next of kin. The mauling of the Bill by the Lords placed the government of the day in a not unexpected position which those unacquainted with English politics believed to be an awkward one. It was awkward in one respect: hanging must cease while the decks were being cleared to conform with democratic ideas. For the first time in history England's hangmen were temporarily unemployed, while the death sentence on the Bill was implemented in order to save the Conservative government's face.

No Hangings: No Increase in Murders!

A curious fact emerged: during this period of no hangings there was neither an increase in the incidence of murder nor was there any noticeable change in the nature of the capital crimes that were being committed! This was an awkward fact to be faced; and boldly the Conservatives faced it—by ignoring it altogether. The resultant compromise was a novel Homicide Act (5 & 6 Eliz. 2 Ch. 11 of 1957). This Act saved not only the Government's face but, more important, it restored hope to wilting hangmen. The Act among other things provides this gem:

> On a charge of murder, it shall be for the defence to prove that the person charged is by virtue of this section not liable to be convicted of murder.

This is a good beginning, but the Act goes on to provide that only certain kinds of murder shall be "capital" murders (that is, liable to the penalty of death by hanging):

> (1) Any murder done in the course of or furtherance of theft.
>
> (2) Any murder by shooting or by causing an explosion.
>
> (3) Any murder done in the course or for the purpose of resisting or avoiding or preventing a lawful arrest, or of effecting or assisting an escape or rescue from legal custody.
>
> (4) Any murder of a police officer acting in the execution of his duty or of a person assisting a police officer so acting.
>
> (5) In the case of a person who was a prisoner at the time when he did or was a party to the murder, any murder of a prison officer acting in the execution of his duty or of a person assisting a prison officer so acting.
>
> (6) Two or more murders on different occasions.

It is not difficult to perceive that these provisions leave scope for hanging; and thus a highly important principle was reaffirmed in a new form. In the excitement and tussle to get this Act passed by the Commons in the form in which it would be acceptable to the Lords, the fact that the Commons had already voted in favour of complete abolition was happily forgotten. Meantime an important hangman, no less a personage than Master Hangman Albert Pierrepoint himself—doyen of England's modern hangmen—had retired: no doubt in some disgust or under the delusion that hanging had been as good as abolished! Such was the immediate effect of this hotch-potch and ill-conceived Act that the campaign against capital punishment in Britain ceased. The strange confusions of the Act soon showed themselves from the moment it became law and Britain's gallows, so to speak, were oiled and dusted for action.

THE NEW SEXUAL OFFENCES ACT

In some ways the Act resembles another wonderful Act of 1959, known as the Sexual Offences Act which, with equally brazen hypocrisy, cleared the main streets of those unfortunates pejoratively labelled "common prostitutes" (in the United States more warmly called "broads") and drove them indoors. This opened new vistas and broader horizons for attractive girls of higher social status and often education who did not fail to take advantage of their openings. They appeared, through a propaganda campaign conducted by bush-telegraph with occult transmitters, under the new names of "call-girls" and "drive-up" girls, who often provided amenities which their less fortunate sisters had been unable to offer: pleasant flats, for example, with central heating and all sorts of real comforts laid on. The call-girls and drive-up girls quickly raised the status of the oldest profession beyond the fondest hopes of those who had the vocation, of those fitted by nature for the call. These brave girls supplied a public need which no citizens appreciated more than the tired and well-to-do man of affairs at a loose end after a gruelling day's work, and with a generous tax-free expenses account at his disposal. It all made good business in many directions and with wide ramifications: for landlords of suitable furnished flats, for hoteliers, restaurateurs, head-waiters, wine-waiters, drinking clubs, and a host of other caterers to the well-being of a humanity with the means to afford the good life. New techniques were developed and many a dull man had to, and did, learn the modern know-how in the ever- developing luxury-jungle of our times. No need to expand this theme, now a commonplace, but it has to be mentioned in order to show how hypocrisy in an Act of Parliament can work out to the advantage of those quick in the uptake. The new Homicide Act meant that a murderer who wished to escape the hangman must fulfil the conditions laid down in the Act: he must avoid the "hanging-murders." The Act left him or her with considerable scope combined with the avoidance of a hanging risk: as, for example, in poisoning; or in throttling, bashing, coshing, or slashing and so forth—providing there was no theft. For all that, the Act did reduce the number of hangings, while retaining the old principle. It also raised other questions.

Campaign for More Hanging: 1960s

It is much too early in the day as these lines are written (in the spring of 1961) to judge fairly the effects of the new Homicide Act. Certain things are definite and can be recorded. In each of the years 1957 and 1958 some 124 murders were known to the police and after the passing of the Act there have been about four hangings each year. It is hardly surprising that some brutal murders, especially of old people and mostly by young or youngish people, provided the hangers with material for propaganda in favour of the reinstitution of capital punishment as it was before the Act. This propaganda, conducted almost entirely by people who believe in retributive punishment, steadily increased. It was reliably polled in early 1960 that not only did about eighty percent of people in general desire a return of corporal punishment for crimes of violence but that about seventy-five percent of the public wanted the judges to be given more powers to hang. The Scottish Tories clamoured for more hangings. He would be a rash man who felt convinced at such a moment that a Tory government with a sweeping majority in the House of Commons would remain passive in the face of so ardent a public opinion! And then there is always the reliable House of Lords. The hangman could well take heart.

ENGLAND'S DEFEAT NOT ALWAYS A VICTORY

Old England's astonishing capacity for mentally looping the loop and thereby enabling her to celebrate military defeats as memorable victories—even giving them a mystical symbolism with an aura of sanctity—all this tradition is sullied by one outstanding exception. After the Parliamentary Bill to reduce hangings to derisory proportions became the law of the land—the defeat and end of a grand old tradition—there were no throwings of bowler hats into the air. Time was when the English people publicly celebrated hangings but, as the reader knows, these celebrations became fewer and fewer as so-called civilization advanced. Now hanging was comparatively rare; and it was all but ignored. The great art was no longer discussed with the fervour of the good old days. Is not this just one more symptom, a sad and pitiable one, of a Great Empire in decline? It is like the closing of the brothels in *la belle France*, where the rot caused by the so-called "progressives" in their anti-French campaigns culminated in this blow against one of the great amenities of French life. But the French, unlike the English, did not lie down under the blow to Liberty, Equality, and Fraternity. They applied their fine intelligence to the problem of *Que faire?* and quickly paid a compliment to another great civilization by adapting the American "call-girl" system to their potent local needs. So it is that today there are in Paris, that Mecca of sexual explorers, hundreds and hundreds of *téléfilles* (as call-girls are so aptly called) at the service of the frustrated, the adventurous, the misunderstood, and the lecherous. I am told, furthermore, that the new system works better than the old— because of the greatly increased discretion and tact of the new generation of superior girls. The only complaints I have heard of are on grounds of greatly increased cost, but in the majority of cases this hardly matters. Such extras can easily be worked into expense accounts; and even charged up for income tax, providing some euphemistic expression is used in the accountancy. There is never any difficulty about this, as any businessman will tell you. And so progress marches on.

Homosexuality in England and France

The year 1960—a memorable one as this book testifies—was also notable for a free debate in Britain's House of Commons on the subject of a recommendation in the findings of a body appointed by the Government to inquire into the laws relating to sexual "offences." Members debated whether a homosexual act between consenting males should continue to be a criminal offence, as it has been for about a century: the English became very pure during Queen Victoria's reign, as all readers of *The Girl with the Swansdown Seat* are aware. In God-fearing England the homo (whether sapiens or otherwise) if caught— sometimes the evidence is by inference only—very often goes to jail. His whole life and livelihood may be ruined. Many think that the punishment is too great. Continental peoples regard homosexuality as *the* English vice, and London as a happy hunting-ground for homosexuals, their own included—as Paris is a happy hunting-ground for heterosexuals of all nationalities, not excluding Limeys and Yanks. At all this the French just smile benevolently. I am reminded of the constant French attitude by an incident which happened in the French Foreign Legion. A legionary—a big, strapping German corporal—was caught out fairly by an orderly sergeant in the very act of a brilliant homosexual performance with a little Levantine private soldier. He was caught at it on a coconut mat in the officers' mess at a base. The orderly sergeant did his duty and brought the offenders before the Commanding Officer, who cross-examined him closely about the circumstances, more out of curiosity than anything else: for such acts are not a crime in either French civil or military law. It came out that the coconut mat was situated below regimental colours and the *tricolore*—the national flag itself. This changed the whole case against the practitioners. The C.O. now felt that he could justly punish the men and he said: "If you have anything further to say, say it now, for your offence is a serious one: *an insult to the flag!*" Whereupon the German corporal pleaded that, in the subdued light of evening, he could not *see* the flag; and he just did not know it was there. The popular little Levantine said that he also did not see the flag and that, had he known it was there, he would most certainly not have behaved as he did. He backed up his companion in a plea of mitigation, and in such moving and patriotic terms that the hardened C.O. was deeply moved. "*Eh bien!*" he said. "Be warned! You must in future choose some other place for play and be sure there are no flags about. You shall be confined to barracks in one cell for the rest of the day. Be off now!" That is an example of French justice for homosexuals. In this case the honour of France was once again saved by intelligence. How different would the outcome have been had this taken place in England! For although London in the 1950s and 1960s has been considered to be Headquarters of the Homosexuals' International and the Mecca of its intelligentsia, it is also the headquarters of English hypocrisy, a much misunderstood word by foreigners, who tend to think that there is something very terrible about being a hypocrite, that is, a person who pretends to be good when he is not. What those foreigners fail to consider are the beams in their own eyes while beholding the motes in the eyes of the English. English hypocrisy is merely a form of English politeness, and is due to the sensitivity of English people.

CONCLUSION

Of the ninety-odd nations representing membership of the United Nations Organization in the year 1961, no fewer than half had abolished the death penalty. If we regard the nations which make up this Organization as what we call the "civilized world," the figure indicates that the civilized world has moved against capital punishment as a means of dealing with criminals—excepting, in certain cases, *political* criminals:

> Treason doth never prosper: what's the reason?
> For if it prosper, none dare call it treason.

—a quotation which must be noted and always kept in mind, even though we are not concerned here with politics but with hanging. If the fact is accepted that a great part of the civilized world is against the execution of criminals for capital crimes, there remain always, as lighthouses in this rocky ocean, Britain and the British Commonwealth and most of the United States of America. The British continue to hang; and so do the Americans in the more enlightened States of the Union. France guillotines, Japan beheads with a sword, Spain garottes, America electrocutes, shoots, gasses, or hangs; and conservative England prefers to hang. Differences in means are accounted for by temperamental differences: the end is the same. Yet murderers are not deterred! English hanging is based on a deeply rooted principle and remains as an ancient and symbolical ritual, not just because execution deters criminals, which cannot be proved. The gallows always has been and still remains for the majority of English Conservatives and for the wider and semi-mystical ruling Establishment in Britain what the violin was to Paganini, what the 'cello has been to Casals, and the piano to Paderewski: a fine instrument and the object of their heart's love. They think of it with deep emotion and look back with nostalgia to Tudor times when Henry VIII hanged his people by the thousand, and to the nineteenth century when a person could be publicly strangled for a theft of five shillings. Those were the days of Merrie England! To such people the abolition of the gallows would be a form of sacrilege, and to them any decline in hanging is a final symptom of the fall of an Empire. There may be setbacks but the mystique of hanging has *not* been exploded. It may remain in the minds of many until the last hydrogen bomb has done its work of educating an obstinate humanity.

We live in an age when government based on force is accepted or tolerated or enforced over the greater part of the earth. But, if events should ever prove that force is not necessary to the happiness and welfare of mankind—and that day may come—then war and capital punishment will disappear. There will be no more hangmen to embellish the romantic concepts of humanity. The hangman's rope, the brass eyelet, the pinions and accoutrements of his great art, the ceremonious ritual of dispatch, the instruments without which there can be no science of government as now accepted: these will disappear.

Those who favour capital punishment and regard hanging as an essential adjunct to their interests and welfare will regard this as a sad prospect for the human race.

They may, nevertheless, take comfort from the fact that it is not yet so; and that whether it will ever be so is highly problematical. The Struldbrugs who order our affairs live on—they seem to be our true immortals. One of them is the public hangman. His place in our culture and civilization is solid and assured, for, even though he should be abolished, the memory of his great contribution to England's place in history will remain in these pages.

VAL

Notes

1. *The Observer*, February 12, 1928.
2. Frazer's *Golden Bough*, iv, page 14.
3. He has since moved to "The Rose and Crown" at Much Hoole on the main Preston road to Southport and Liverpool.
4. *A Spy Has No Friend*, by Ronald Seth (1952).
5. If any.
6. See Mr. Berry's apologia, page 221.
7. Home Office instructions to Prison Governors read at the Old Bailey, 15/12/1926.

    In 1956 Lord Mancroft, Under-Secretary, Home Office, added to this. Now (1961) where there is a hitch at a hanging, Governors must report to the H.O., which keeps a record.
8. In the year 1960—a generation after this journalistic scoop—a comstockian commentator wrote that, even in the American Yellow Press, it was "still considered the basement-level of pictorial journalism."
9. A scientific friend points out that "squelch" should read "dull plonk."
10. See Annual Criminal Statistics, England and Wales.
11. *The Observer* (16/4/1961): "An Analysis of Murder" by Dr. Terence Morris and Louis Blom-Cooper. I am greatly indebted to this thought-provoking analysis.
12. See pp.67–68 for abolitionist list. All other states retain death penalty.
13. Mr. (afterwards Sir) Joynson Hicks and later Lord Brentford—familiarly known as Jix.
14. See *Hansard* (House of Commons) for 28/1/1953.
15. In 1961 this became so threatening that extra noughts may be required by the time it is read.

16. Many books have since appeared on the subject, none better than Roy Calvert's.

17. This *et seq.* is taken from the *News of the World*, 29 August, 1923.

18. Emrys Hughes in *Tribune* (4/5/1956), from which words in inverted commas in this paragraph are quoted. The proprieties observed did not prevent the onlookers' anguish.

19. *Peter the Great* (1929).

20. *The History of Ireland*, by John Mitchel, Vol. I, page 482.

21. Edmund About, *Greece and the Greeks*.

22. *Quevedo's Works* (Routledge, 1925). Excellently edited and translated by myself. —C.D.

23. Computed from the newspapers cited. Approximate figures. The *Daily News* became the *News Chronicle*, to close down in 1960. The *Daily Telegraph* absorbed the *Morning Post*. *Lloyds Sunday News* also closed down.

24. Quoted from the *New Republic*, 25th January, 1928.

25. See *The New Statesman and Nation* (21/4/1956), article, "The Pierrepoint Papers" by Reginald Reynolds. I have quoted very briefly from these classics.

26. *Tribune* (4/5/1956) article by Emrys Hughes.

27. In 1953 there was much public controversy over THREE cases in which innocent men may have been hanged: Derek Bentley, in 1953, Timothy Evans, in 1950, and Walter Rowland, in 1948. See *Hanged and Innocent* (published by Gollancz, 1953), and *Ten Rillington Place* by Ludovic Kennedy (1960).

28. Dr. Frederic Gaertner.

29. Gules (from French *goules* = ermine dyed red). Here it means "red" (in description of armorial bearings). —C.D.

30. This information is based upon that rare and interesting book: *History of the Guillotine*, by the Right Hon. John Wilson Croker (John Murray, 1853). Some authorities say that the first all-French guillotine was made by a Dr. Louis and used in 1792. I am told that during their occupation of France in World War I the Nazis used an electric guillotine. I still await confirmation. —CD.

31. Professor L.G.V. Rota, quoted in the *Daily Mail*, 14th January, 1928.

32. *Sing Sing Doctor*. By Amos O. Squire.

33. *Scottisboro Boy*. By Haywood Patterson and Earl Conrad.

34. In the U.S.A. the letter "z" is pronounced "zee," so this would be *zee-zee-zee*, which sounds nicer than *izz-izz-izz*, etc.

35. An honorary title, conferred by the popular press.

36. Now Lord Birkett.

37. He has since moved—see footnote 3.

38. 5/12/1947.

39. *Bygone Punishments*, by W. Andrews.

40. With five applications for the post every week.

41. *My Experiences as an Executioner*, from which all the facts about the late Mr. Hangman Berry and *his* art are quoted.

42. The formula is as given by Mr. Berry, who no doubt gave it incorrectly in order to preserve his secret. —C.D.

43. Mr. Berry was a most methodical man. There is a chapter of his book on "The Business Side of Hanging." He kept his accounts very carefully.

44. The consistency of the figures in the Berry Table has often been queried. The final answer is that, right or wrong, they *always* worked in practice. See footnote 42.

45. See pages 47–48, 137–139.

46. See *Ready Reckoner for Hangmen*, Appendix.

47. i.e., partly by mental arithmetic.

48. As will be seen, Dr. Barr later made amends.

49. An officious busybody, no doubt.

50. This generous testimony is quoted to show the magnanimity of Dr. Barr. The reader will obtain from this long quotation from Mr. Berry's book an extraordinarily fine picture of the mentality of a hangman, and will realize what a matter-of-fact view of the business is taken. The testimony, it will be noted, refers to one Peter Cassidy and not to John Conway.

51. White, to distinguish it from the judge's black cap. The judge mourns, the hangman rejoices.

52. Owing to public demonstrations outside prisons likely to obstruct traffic, etc., it has been found necessary to vary the hour: 9 a.m. is now fashionable.

53. Note Mr. Berry's eye for detail.

54. Cmd. 8932, H.M. Stationery Office, 12s. 6d. net.

APPENDIX

A READY RECKONER FOR HANGMEN

RULE.—Take the weight of the Client in Stones and look down the column of weights until you reach the figures nearest to 24 cwt., and the figure in the left-hand column will be the DROP.

(Each cell is given as cwt · qr · lb.)

Distance falling in feet.	8 Stone	9 Stone	10 Stone	11 Stone	12 Stone	13 Stone	14 Stone	15 Stone	16 Stone	17 Stone	18 Stone	19 Stone
Zero	8 0 0	9 0 0	10 0 0	11 0 0	12 0 0	13 0 0	14 0 0	15 0 0	16 0 0	17 0 0	18 0 0	19 0 0
1 ft.	11 1 15	12 2 23	14 0 14	15 2 4	16 3 22	18 1 12	19 3 2	21 0 21	22 2 11	24 0 1	25 1 19	26 3 9
2 ft.	13 3 16	15 2 15	17 1 14	19 0 12	20 3 11	22 2 9	24 1 8	26 0 7	27 3 5	29 2 4	31 1 2	33 0 1
3 ft.	16 0 0	18 0 0	20 0 0	22 0 0	24 0 0	26 0 0	28 0 0	30 0 0	32 0 0	34 0 0	36 0 0	38 0 0
4 ft.	17 2 11	19 3 5	22 0 0	24 0 22	26 3 22	28 2 11	30 3 5	33 0 0	35 0 22	37 0 16	39 2 11	41 3 15
5 ft.	19 2 11	22 0 5	24 2 0	26 3 22	29 1 16	31 3 11	34 1 5	36 3 0	39 0 22	41 2 16	44 0 11	46 2 5
6 ft.	21 0 22	23 3 11	26 2 0	29 0 16	31 3 5	34 1 22	37 0 11	39 3 0	41 2 16	45 0 5	47 2 22	50 1 11
7 ft.	22 2 22	25 2 4	28 1 14	31 3 5	34 1 22	37 0 11	39 3 0	42 2 7	45 1 16	48 0 5	50 3 15	53 3 26
8 ft.	24 0 11	27 0 12	30 0 14	34 0 5	36 3 15	39 3 15	42 0 19	45 2 7	48 0 22	51 0 23	54 0 25	57 0 26
9 ft.	25 1 5	28 1 23	31 2 14	36 0 16	37 3 22	42 0 19	44 1 2	47 1 21	50 2 11	53 3 1	56 3 19	60 0 9
10 ft.	26 2 4	29 3 11	33 0 19	37 3 22	39 3 5	43 0 13	46 1 20	49 3 0	53 0 7	56 1 15	59 2 22	63 0 2